(Continued)

UNCOMMON CARING

Learning from Men Who Teach Young Children

James R. King

Teachers College, Columbia University
New York and London

Published by Teachers College Press, 1234 Amsterdam Avenue, New York, NY 10027

Library of Congress Cataloging-in-Publication Data

King, James R., 1952–
   Uncommon caring : learning from men who teach young children /
James R. King.
      p.   cm. — (Early childhood education series)
   Includes bibliographical references (p.   ) and index.
   ISBN 0-8077-3740-2 (cloth : alk. paper). — ISBN 0-8077-3739-9
(pbk. : alk. paper)
   1. Male primary school teachers—United States.   2. Male primary
school teachers—United States—Attitudes.   3. Sex differences in
education—United States.   I. Title.   II. Series: Early childhood
education series (Teachers College Press)
LB1775.8.K56   1998
372.11—dc21   98-3464

ISBN 0-8077-3739-9 (paper)
ISBN 0-8077-3740-2 (cloth)

Printed on acid-free paper

Manufactured in the United States of America

05   04   03   02   01   00   99   98   8   7   6   5   4   3   2   1

Contents

Preface

Male primary teachers are those men who teach in the first 4 years of schooling. Kindergarten, first-, second-, and third-grade teachers spend most of their days with young children during what are, some would argue, the most important and formative years of schooling. In this challenging and rewarding effort, men are almost nonexistent. As a teacher educator in elementary and early childhood, and as a former first-, second-, and third-grade teacher, I had personal theories about my uniqueness as a male primary teacher. However, to better understand our patterned underrepresentation ("the lower you go [in grades], the less likely you'll find a man"), I participated in a study with a group of men who do teach primary school, and who, at the beginning of the study, were teaching in grades K–3. The study began as an interview follow-up to a survey. But somewhere in the course of the interviews, we began functioning more as a study group, with me as one of the learners. I received clippings, articles, and other artifacts. I was invited into classrooms, asked for my opinion, and sat down and talked to. Eventually we began to discover that we talked about some things repeatedly. We returned to issues that related to teaching as caring, teaching as gendered behavior, and the relationship of sexual orientation and teachers' suitability.

These topics became the themes for this book, which is organized in three parts. Part I introduces the themes and the framework for the study. Chapter 1 is an overview of the issues that surround men's work with children in primary grade classrooms. In this chapter I examine men's avoidance of primary education from the perspectives of role definition, feminist analysis of economic factors, and prestige hierarchies. Chapter 2 describes primary teaching as a female culture, with grounding in Jennifer Nias's (1989) description of British primary (elementary) teachers, Nel Noddings's (1984, 1992) constructs of teaching as acts of caring, and Carol Gilligan's (1982) theory of women's moral positioning. In Chapter 3, I describe my study with the male primary teachers, provide contextual details, and briefly introduce the participants.

Part II presents stories written by participants in the study. Paul wrote Chapter 4 after a difficult semester as an undergraduate teacher education student. Chapter 5 is Steve's recollection of his "coming to know" primary teaching culture. Ken's personal experiences of being torn between caring for his students and (quietly) caring for his dying partner are related in Chapter 6. Chapter 7 presents Gregg's thoughts on primary teaching as gendered behavior. In Chapter 8, Cal critiques the practice of relying on text as mediated curriculum in the primary grades. Chapter 9 is a simulated interview between Evan and myself. In it he critiques teaching culture and the women who work within it.

In Part III, I analyze the major themes that emerged during the interviews, from the men's writings, and from focus group discussions with the male primary teachers. Each chapter is written around quotes and vignettes from the data and concludes with a synthesis of others' writings that are related to the main theme(s) of each chapter. In Chapter 10, men's use of and reaction to teaching as caring are detailed. Women's ways of teaching (as caring) are beliefs and strategies that the men simultaneously approximated and devalued. Critiques of care as a way of understanding women's work are also offered. Chapter 11 details the negotiations the men made *as men* working in a feminine context. It is gender work. While some "women's ways" were seen as simply good teaching, others were seen as impediments to teaching because they were female. In Chapter 12, men's sexual orientations are discussed as they are thought to affect their appropriateness for teaching. Chapter 13 reexamines the three themes of care, gender, and sexual orientation for their interactive effects on the men who choose to teach in primary grades.

After this experience with seven teachers, I realize that we have begun something that still begs for more attention. The culture's constructions of "teacher" and "male" both hold a great deal of potential energy. Unpacking the beliefs is continuing work. I am grateful to the "primary males" who helped me understand myself a little more clearly.

This book results from the participation and support of many people. I am grateful to the University of South Florida for a grant from the Research and Creative Scholarship Program. I am also indebted to three school districts for their support during the study that informs this manuscript. Several people read, provided feedback and direction, as well as support during the writing of this book: Laurie MacGillivray, Donna Avermann, Jenifer Schneider, Roger Brindley, Mary Alice Barksdale-Ladd, Bena Hefflin, Kathy Oropallo, Jane Young, and Linda Lopez-McAllister. Several other readers were generous with comments at crucial moments: Jonathan Silin, Joe Tobin, Valerie Walkerdine, and Michael Kimmel. During the production of the manuscript, I received helpful guidance from Susan Liddicoat and editorial help from Peter Sieger. Finally, much of this book was written at the kitchen table, often with my partner, Richard, watching from across the counter. Every time I asked "Does this make sense?" he listened as I read aloud and then offered his response. This book is for Richard Alvarez.

PART I

A Study of Men's Care, Gender, and Teaching in the Primary Grades

CHAPTER 1

Uncommon Caring

Teaching, particularly teaching in the primary grades, has been construed as an act of caring. Primary grade teachers whom I know often say, "We teach the child, not the subject." Teaching the child requires teachers who can address affective, emotional processes as well as cognitive ones. More specifically, teachers are intentionally seen as filling in for missing family members or functions. And in these times when prototypes for traditional families may no longer be representative of schoolchildren's home lives, there is a resuscitation of the call for men to participate in teaching at the primary grade level. Presumably, male teachers are thought to provide some missing family structure by virtue of their gender. Yet, even with this renewed invitation, men are not choosing to become primary teachers—a pattern that is grounded in culturally constructed factors such as attitudes toward caring, gender-coded behavior, and sexual orientations. The major purpose of this book is to explore these issues as a response to the query, Why do so few men choose to teach in primary grade classrooms?

A public perception is that men who teach primary grades are often either homosexuals, pedophiles, or principals in training. These commonly held, but seldom voiced, presuppositions have had a strong impact on men's decisions about whether to teach young children. Furthermore, such perceptions ensure that the men who do choose to be primary teachers are frequently seen as "suspect." While the rhetoric from the educational institutions overtly entices young men to consider elementary teaching, we covertly monitor those male teachers who aren't married and who "act funny." At this point, I do not intend to speak against the careful monitoring of who is and who is not encouraged or allowed to teach children, for I believe it is crucial to evaluate prospective teachers' suitability for work with young children. Yet, as a primary teacher, a teacher mentor, and a gay man, I wish to examine some of the frameworks that have been used in the covert monitoring of male primary school teachers and to suggest that some evaluation frameworks for prospective and current teachers are misguided. When primary education is viewed in a context of caring, men's work as

3

caregivers can be seen as a problem. This chapter examines some of the relationships among caring, masculinity, work roles, and children.

UNCOMMON MEN IN A CONTEXT OF CARE

Teaching in the primary grades is a complex endeavor. Nias (1989) describes the experience as one that requires teachers who are comfortable teaching from their personal values, most especially "caring for" and "loving" children. While caring is an important part of teaching at all levels, love and care as well as other nurturing behaviors are privileged attributes in primary teaching contexts. One could even say care is requisite for, or synonymous with, primary teaching. Care is, of course, not the only noteworthy aspect of primary grade teaching. There is content knowledge and pedagogic translation of that knowledge into classroom activity. Teachers routinely observe and assess their students and classrooms for the data that drive their decision making, as well as rely on professional knowledge about children and their development. These knowledge bases are not discrete, but interactive. It is certainly not my intention to essentialize all primary teaching as a domain devoid of intellectual or abstract reasoning. My experience suggests the contrary. Rather, I am focusing on the attribute of caring, which appears to be, at least in popular culture and in educational folklore, situated in early years teaching.

For many, attributions of care have tended to shape (or been shaped by) a public perception of primary teaching as "women's work." When teaching is construed as an act of caring, then care as a gender-identified behavior has extra significance. In fact, Noddings (1992) writes, "Women have learned to regard every human encounter as a potential caring occasion" (p. 24). I interpret Noddings to mean that caring is essentialized as a feminine way of relating to or constructing social realities. When primary teaching is read as caring, and caring signifies a female way of knowing, men who choose to teach in these classrooms may be at risk.

The men who enter primary teaching do so with a quasi-remedial designation. As with any stigma, the whole person becomes framed by the conspicuous mark (Goffman, 1963). In fact, caring enacted by men receives explicitly negative marking. The conflating of caring and primary teaching has had predictable effects on men's participation. A survey reported by the National Association for the Education of Young Children (NAEYC; 1985) suggests that only about 5% of direct child-care providers were men. A subsequent study completed in 1993 by the National Center for the Early Childhood Workforce revealed that men continue to teach in small numbers in early childhood centers. The study reported that 3% of direct child-care teachers are male (Whitebook, Phillips, & Howes, 1993). Given these low percentages and the persistence of the pattern, it is crucial to remember that there is no systematic evidence suggesting that men are inappropriate persons to provide the nurturing and caring that are thought to be essential for learning contexts that involve preschool children. Further, when one considers the analogously low representation of men who teach in the primary grades, similar questions arise. In the study that underlies this book, men comprised less than 1% of the primary teachers. Therefore it is important to examine how it might be that men are so dramatically underrepresented in the profession of primary education.

WHY MEN IGNORE THE CALL TO TEACH

Seifert (1988) has suggested that men's experience as fathers means that they can successfully engage in caring and nurturing behaviors. Even so, he is careful to point out that the caring provided by men as fathers is at least differentiated from that provided by teachers in the limited length of fixed units of time spent caring for their children. Teachers are required to care for children over much longer intervals than are fathers. It is also quite possible that fathers fill the role of number-two care giver, often as a helper or a supplement to mothers. In caring, male classroom teachers are on their own. Perhaps recognizing these differences in caring, men, Seifert reasons, more readily choose other work alternatives. Since they characteristically have greater numbers of employment options, men more readily choose those options in preference to early childhood teaching.

Seifert further suggests that the reasoning behind the rhetoric, "We need more men teaching primary grades," may also be problematic and that it negatively influences men's selection of primary teaching. His first argument is a "compensation hypothesis," which simultaneously suggests that men can provide "sex-appropriate" role models for boys *and* offer children of both sexes models of caring, nurturing men. But Seifert sees these two issues as contradictory. It is quite possible that a sensitive, nurturing man could be perceived by others, most notably parents, as providing a role model that is inappropriate for young boys. Some parents may not want their children exposed to nurturing, caring, or what the parents may construe as "soft" males. This paradox of gender-inscribed social behavior as it relates to sexual orientation is examined in Chapter 12. For now, suffice to say that perhaps the role ambiguity inherent in male caring and the confusion that results from disrupting the expected gender-related social behaviors have contributed to some men's decisions not to be primary teachers. Seifert's (1988) second argument, a "social equity hypothesis," proposes that men entering primary teaching may enhance the stature of what is perceived to be "women's work." This, too, is a problematic assumption that entails the notion of "women's work," as I explore in the next section.

TEACHING AS "WOMEN'S WORK"

Seifert's discussion of gender bias regarding society's construction of both "early childhood teacher" and "primary grade teacher" as female is important to the discussion of choosing to be a primary grade teacher. We systematically direct male students away from the primary grades (Seifert, 1983). Teachers also gender-type teacher's roles according to traditional perceptions of gender. Seeing primary education as "women's work" is problematic for many reasons. First of all, recent feminist perspectives propose that nurturing and caring (Noddings, 1992) or connected knowing (Belenky, Clinchy, Goldberger, & Tarule, 1986) are strengths that are particular, though not exclusive, to women's (and girls') experiences in our culture. So in one sense, being female can be seen as predisposing one to primary education when teaching, especially primary teaching, is seen as caring (Noddings, 1984). My interpretation is that the intent of this feminist essentialist reasoning is to create an understanding of women's perceptions and theories of the world and how those constructs might differ from a male perspective. Yet, when that same femininist model of knowing and being is mapped into patriarchal institutions, such as schools, contradictory messages emerge. In fact, the special characteristics accorded women in these recent feminist epistemologies have also been used to devalue women's job skill and expertise in hierarchically organized and competitive workplaces. According to Reskin (1991):

> Women's assignment to child care, viewed as unskilled work in our society, illustrates these patterns. Women are said to have a "natural talent" for it and similar work; men are relieved from doing it; society obtains free or cheap child care; and women are handicapped from competing with men. (p. 147)

If nurturing and caring are "skills" that are rewarded inside the professions of child care and teaching, they are also devalued outside these professions. Sugg (1978) has suggested that American education generally, and teaching particularly have been systematically feminized and, as a result, have lost status. Like other writers during this time, Sugg spoke for a return to the male influences that had prevailed at the turn of the twentieth century. Unlike Sugg, I do not wish for a return to traditional, reclamationist curricula and teacher "roles." In fact, I scrupulously avoid advocating what *should* happen. But I do think an examination of sexist devaluing of teaching is appropriate—for all teaching. Because others outside early childhood education, including teachers at other levels, see our requisite skilled behaviors as "natural" or as feminine predispositions, they may not feel compelled to reward those competencies with appropriate compensation. Or since child-care job skills are acquired prior to their execution at the work site, the skills themselves are seen as "natural" and therefore neither technical nor job-specific. Again, economic reward is unnecessary.

With different intents, the arguments of Reskin (1991) and Sugg (1978) share common ground in describing and providing explanations for women's marginalized status as teachers. Sugg suggests that "motherteacher" was a construct based on a "pedagogy of love" that built a "cult of the child, sanctified 'growth,' undermined the values of tradition and maturity, and further subverted the curriculum and with it, the authority of teachers" (p. xi). Sugg's remedies for such incursions into authority were a common school curriculum, a standardized theory of instruction, and balanced representation of the sexes. The arguments regarding the culture of teaching that were proposed by Sugg read, on first gloss, disturbingly like my own.

Sugg's arguments call for a reinstated "masculine" presence in education. For the primary grades, the proposal might sound (and has sounded) like "We need more men in early childhood to provide masculine influence." A circular argument such as this does not examine what the desire is actually instantiating. More succinctly, what is it about masculinity that we claim to want for these young children?

Robinson (1981) provided a more systematic look at the culture's desire to locate men in early childhood and primary grade education. For the 1940s and 1950s, Robinson reports a virtual prohibition of men working with young children. Men were "not in their element" and would most certainly "be suspect" (p. 27, citing Tubbs, 1946). Neither Tubbs nor, subsequently, Robinson named the underlying suspicions. The unnamed, silent accusation of pedophilia lurks, ready to fill in the purposive blanks in the discourse on permissible teachers.

In the 1960s and 1970s, Robinson reports a shift toward "what men could contribute" to teaching in the lower grades. Traditionalists in the 1960s and 1970s, fearing the production of feminized boys in an exclusively female-dominated educational/social context, called for greater numbers of men in elementary education. In particular, Smith (1973) suggested that young boys were harmed by an exclusively feminine environment in elementary school. Brophy and Good (1973b) countered Smith's argument with the notion that culturally learned social and gender roles, as they were/are deployed in classrooms, caused the feminization of education and, thereby, children. In fact, the presence of a man in a classroom apparently made little difference from Brophy and Good's (1973a) perspective. In a later extensive review of the research on male teachers and student outcomes, Gold and Reis (1982) support the conclusions of Brophy and Good. Yet Brophy and Good stop short of asking whether or not "feminization" might be a productive shift within education. And, in general, the calls for examination of the culture of early education at this time did not critique the masculinist assumptions that were presumably being eroded by female teachers.

To a limited degree Robinson (1981) engages with gender-based expectations in his third stage of men's participation in early education from the late 1970s to the early 1980s, which he calls the age of androgyny. Again, with hindsight, it is easy to critique and suggest that we have yet to move toward androgyny, if in fact it ever was a shared goal. The genders remain separately ensconced. Yet Robinson and colleagues (Robinson, 1981, 1979; Robinson & Canaday, 1978; Robinson & Flake-Hobson, 1979; Robinson, Sheen, & Flake-Hobson, 1978) argue for an androgyny that he maintains will equip male teachers "to soothe the hurt feelings" and "enable men as well as women to involve children in playing ball" (Robinson, 1981, p. 30). Robinson concludes that "highly masculine men would feel uncomfortable, threatened, or incapable of following through on the traditionally feminine aspects of an early education teacher's day" (p. 30). So, desirable men are able to perform women's work and not be threatened doing so. And female teachers are asked (once again) to play ball. Androgynous male teachers are considered by Robinson a good bet. I am tempted to agree and move on. But Robinson does not question the culture to which these special males must apprentice. Nor does he question the suitability of the work for all teachers, including women.

Almost inadvertently, Robinson quotes Podolner's address at the Male Caucus of the 1978 NAEYC:

> And I want him (my son) to know that he as a man can contribute equally to the joyous task of rearing young children without threatening his masculinity— quite the contrary, that he will only become a man when he doesn't need the facade of masculinity to prevent him from being fully human (p. 2). (quoted in Robinson, 1981, p. 31)

For me, Podolner's oppositional construction of masculinity and humanity begins to reveal the complexity of males retrofitting as primary grade teachers. Using oppositional binaries brings to my mind Foucault's (1972) use of "what is not" to reveal the truth of "what is." In the case of primary teaching, we so consistently talk about what it is (caring) to conceal what it cannot be (male). While the truth behind these binaries is that there is no consistent relationship, we seldom look beneath the discourse to see why it is being deployed. In his deconstructive flourish, Podolner goes to the root metaphor (Sarbin, 1983) and reveals patriarchal masculinity as the problem. My hunch, again based on the advantage afforded by historical perspective, is that a negative predisposition toward hegemonic masculinity was a theme in this address. Later, such talk would be called "male-bashing," and a sequestering of that argument to academic papers, or a silence of dismissal, crept up on such educational discourses that were critical of male privilege. Robinson's (1986) later summary provides a more updated view of his earlier proposals about androgynous male teachers for young children. Again, he concludes with a cloaked discussion of pedophilic accusations that haunt male teachers of young children and may dissuade others from becoming primary teachers.

Arguments relative to gender typing and sex-segregated work are also helpful in understanding the small numbers of men for reasons other than compensation for work. To return to Reskin (1991), dominant groups (men) maintain their economic advantages by differentiating work, and they support that advantage through physical segregation and behavioral differentiation. Since "difference" is a necessary presupposition for dominance, physically segregating men and women is necessary. Reskin proposes that men actively keep men and women in different working contexts because working as equals minimizes perceived differences and threatens to reduce the dominance of men. Social-task differentiation by gender also preserves males' hegemonic positions. Reskin suggests that when women and men do work in the same physical and psychological space, equal pay for equal work is a more plausible outcome.

Of course, women who teach are rewarded more equitably in relation to men who teach than they might be in less gender-integrated professions. However, when salary schedules for public school teachers are differentiated by grade levels, elementary teachers make less money than either secondary teachers or "specialists." So while primary teachers do better than women's 60 cents to each dollar of men's pay, they may still be a "good buy" for the culture. Allowing men to participate in elementary culture may cause a shift in prestige and salary for both men *and women* in primary and preschool contexts (Seifert, 1988). In order to reduce the likelihood of that possibility, the social construction of "primary teacher" has been loaded with features that surround the constructs of "female" and "mother." Our culture defines primary teacher and mother very similarly. Given the implicit fear of "the feminine" and misogynistic responses to that fear, men will be dissuaded from primary teaching. In contrast, arguing from Tronto's (1993) stance, men who do decide to teach in primary grades are joining a culture that has already circumscribed itself as one that is axiomatically of less value. I understand the issue as one that is more pervasive than the gender of the participants. Entering the culture of primary education means entering a feminine culture and tacitly agreeing to conform to its norms, irrespective of gender—a challenge for men *and* women.

When a male *does* choose to break the social taboo of working *with* women, there are serious consequences to be paid. The category of "male primary teacher" has been so crafted that it implicitly includes negative, low-prestige features, such as "feminine," "homosexual," and "pedophile." These cultural and semantic loadings on the "male primary teacher" are, in my opinion, the reason the voices of these professionals are muted. And with silence, we lose the chance to interrogate those unspoken accusations. I am suggesting that these associations, construed negatively by the culture, are being used to control the number of men who choose to enter primary education and to manipulate those men who do teach young children. Further, it is apparent that the appropriation of the constructs "feminine," "homosexual," and "pedophile" reveals much about the misogyny and heterosexism implicit in these devaluing comparisons. It is also important to realize that these same dynamics have been reported in other female-dominated professions. When men attempt to enter other female professions, similar results occur.

NURSING: A PARALLEL EXAMPLE

Like the men who teach in the primary grades, men who choose to enter the field of nursing must expect that their motives and suitabilities for nursing will be questioned. Hesselbart's (1977) analysis of the role of men in the nursing profession parallels the reasoning about men who teach in elementary grades. The comparison suggests that elementary education, nursing, and other professions dominated by women offer a glimpse into the intersection of gender and work. According to Hesselbart (1977), men in the field of nursing compete on a level with women. In that effort, they imitate a group with less ascribed status (women) and therefore appear deviant. In a study of male nurses as status contradiction, B. Segal (1962) reached the same conclusion: "In our society, the male winner of a competition with women has but a shallow victory." . . . "It is more or less unrespectable to a man and hence damaging to his prestige and self esteem to be a member of the nursing profession, an occupation in which a large majority of the job incumbents are women" (p. 37, 32).

More succinctly, Schreiber (1979) points out the restricted role possibilities in this competition. "The male nurse is [thought] either 'queer' or driven to the top of the heap" (p. 24). Men aren't considered successful in women's work until they are in a position of authority over women. Yet the conquest itself is fraught with questions of value. And even when male nurses learn to be comfortable with their career choices, others are not so sanguine. Lynn, Vaden, and Vaden (1975) report that female doctors embarrass male patients; male nurses embarrass female patients and are "considered suspect by male patients" (p. 5). Bradley (1993) adds that it is easier for women to push into men's jobs than it is for men to work in women's jobs: "The threat to masculinity in entering a women's area is much greater because of the [men's] greater visibility and possible stigmatization of male homosexuality" (p. 14). The conclusions reached by Lynn and colleagues (1975) are not promising: "Public attitudes challenging the masculinity of men entering traditionally female occupations undoubtedly have created and will continue to create a formidable barrier" (p. 11).

To better understand the influence of sex-role stereotyping in primary teaching, a discussion of the social construction of teachers' permissible and gender-coded behaviors is presented in the following chapter on teaching as care and female. From the discussion in this chapter, it is clear that stereotyped attributions for men who choose female-dominated careers are common and more generalized than the example of primary grade teaching.

CHAPTER 2

Teaching = Caring = Female

Historically, teaching in the early grades is a profession that has been sustained by women. Teaching in primary grades occurs in a complex culture that is female, even feminine, but decidedly nonfeminist. Nias (1989) describes the experience as one that requires teachers who are comfortable teaching from their personal values, most especially "caring for" and "loving" children. While caring is an important part of teaching at all levels, love and care, as well as other nurturing behaviors, are privileged attributes of primary teaching. Care is requisite or synonymous with primary teaching. Teaching as caring is accomplished by primary teachers in ways that are perhaps different from those of other teachers. Primary teachers are described by Nias as teaching in integrated ways, including both curriculum and relationships. That is, primary teachers integrate subject areas such as math, science, and literacy into cohesive, inclusive learning activities. Similarly, primary teachers interact with students, as well as with other teachers, in ways that build and maintain close relationships and with a sense of connectedness. So, integration occurs in primary teachers' subject areas and their personal relationships.

I agree with Nias's characterizations of teaching in the primary grades as integration and suggest that the dichotomy of academic subjects and interpersonal relationships is likewise one that is imploded, causing an even more thorough integration. So, subject-area boundaries are breached, and interpersonal relationships are part of the class curriculum. Integration of academic subjects and relationships leads to teaching in ways that hinge on teachers' affiliation with reference groups. These social groups are formed among colleagues, with students, and across levels of school hierarchy, as well as outside of schools' social contexts.

The caring and nurturing that characterize the culture of primary education are themes that parallel feminist views of females' moral development (Gilligan, 1982), feminist accounts of caring (Noddings, 1984), and women's ways of learning and knowing (Belenky et al., 1986). In fact, Noddings's *Caring: A Feminine Approach to Ethics and Moral Education* (1984) and Nias's *Primary Teachers Talking* (1989), have much in common in their conceptualization of teaching as acts of caring. To better understand how teaching in the primary grades might be viewed as a caring context, I present each of these positions about caring and when appropriate make applications to teaching in primary grades.

TEACHING AS CARING

Noddings (1984) makes the case that acts of teaching are special instances of moral and ethical relationships, which she interprets as "caring." These caring acts are between the one caring (teacher) and the one cared for (students). While these social arrangements are not attributed by Noddings exclusively to teachers, it is significant that most of the discussion is related to teaching relationships. Noddings suggests that entering the profession of teaching is to enter a "very special—and specialized—caring relationship" (p. 174). She characterizes teachers' (the one caring) professional moves as ones centered on students (the cared for). "When a teacher asks a question in class and a student responds, the teacher receives not just the 'response' but the student [as well]" (p. 176). The answer is less important than the engagement between the student and the teacher. According to Noddings, teachers accomplish their focus on students by "be[ing] totally and *nonselectively* present to the student—each student—as he addresses me" (p. 180; emphasis added). Offering oneself nonselectively to each (and all) students on individual bases presupposes teachers have constructed, or continue to build, relationships with each student. "Being there" includes elements of empathic identification with the students who need their teacher. Teachers' caring relationships with their students, then, are the context that guides being their teacher and a being-there teacher.

Noddings extends the metaphor of teaching as care in *The Challenge to Care in Schools: An Alternative Approach to Education* (1992). While the subtitle offers caring as an alternative, the challenge remains. Noddings's ambiguity in the title is potentially revealing. The challenge could be one offered to teachers. This is the challenge (to teachers) to care in schools. The implication is that teachers should care, a view stated more directly by Henderson and Bibens (1970). And, if found not to be caring in their teaching, these teachers are marked. Yet it is subjective and individual work when we build a relationship based on what we construe as care. Individual teachers' interpretations of "caring" acts are likely to be very different when their interpretations are based on their individual experiences of being cared for and providing care for others. Teaching in caring ways becomes *the* model, and some of us must become "challenged care providers" or remedial caregivers. On a personal level, Noddings challenges me to be a caring teacher. It is problematic to issue such a challenge to care.

Another interpretation fixes the challenge to care on the construct itself. I might ask, Can a theory of care transform teaching (that is presumably without care)? It seems to me that this is a much more pervasive indictment of teaching as a potentially noncaring construct. In *The Challenge to Care in Schools*, Noddings (1992) maintains the ideas developed in *Caring*. In teaching as caring, the connection requires that two human beings transact the caring relationship. The "one caring" (teacher) and the "cared for" (student) both participate in enacting an instance of care. The one caring is again described in *The Challenge to Care in Schools* as using "open, non-selective receptivity to[ward] the cared for" (p. 15). Noddings invokes a spiritual motif and suggests that the "soul" of the one caring (the teacher) "empties itself of its own content in order to receive the other" (p. 16). I understand this metaphor of the teachers' spirit as Nodding's description of an empathic response by teachers to children's needs, as those needs are perceived by the teacher. It is clear from Noddings that students' needs are not simply cognitive or academic ones but include interpersonal, spiritual, and moral needs as well. Being a "being there/their teacher" is a taxing path. The intent is to respond in helpful or appropriate ways to each of our students. To me, this stance requires that as a teacher I be capable of being a different person in response to each instantiation of "their needs." While it is potentially rich and rewarding, being their teacher seems simultaneously an endless and draining demand. And in response to the resource commitment to caring, Noddings offers the theoretical construct of care. The question remains: Is care a sufficiently resilient and comprehensive enough frame to support such a demanding effort?

If teachers attempt to respond to children through a therapeutic medium of their perceptions of students' needs, then teachers' abilities to be aware, to make empathic judgments, and negotiate the balance between "curriculum press" and emotional support are crucial. In the phrase "curriculum press," I am referring to teachers' internalized awareness of curriculum, tasks, and lessons that, at some level of their consciousness, they know they must cover at some level of (teacher) completeness or (student) mastery. It is teachers' constant mental volley between what should be done, as determined by curriculum press, and their attention to students' needs that consumes teachers.

Noddings (1992) suggests "When I care, I really hear, see, or feel what the other tries to convey" (p. 16). While Noddings suggests that caring is a way of being in a relation and not a set of specific behaviors, I remain ambivalent. First, there is much to agree with here. Teaching as caring, promoted as a perspective toward our work, is promising. Such a stance begins to unpack the multiple moralities of choices embedded in the decisions that teachers make in a minute-by-minute adjudication of the trials in their classrooms. It is clear that cost-benefit analysis, dispensing justice, and honoring individualism, the universe of Kohlberg's (1981) male morality, are only small parts of teachers' construction of "a classroom." In addition to justice-informed morality, being part of a family, the feelings of family members and friends, and our individual and shared histories of interactions are but a few of the relational issues that round out our formations of the moralities that inform our choices. Yet I am simultaneously wary that caring, as defined by Noddings, or by another theorist, or by a principal who is pressured to "implement caring," will cause caring to become another set of teacher pressures. As Noddings (1992) writes (perhaps portentously), "teachers not only *have to* create caring relations in which they are the carers, but they also *have a responsibility* to help students develop the capacity to care" (p. 18; emphasis added). It is, from my moral stance, a position that is comfortable. But I am tentative that *my* vision of my personal relationship with my students would be promoted as *the* relationship/teaching model. Nevertheless, teaching as caring is a pervasive, though largely unexamined, metaphor for primary teaching.

While Noddings addresses these arguments to the ethics of teaching in general, I suggest that they are particularly well suited to the culture of primary teaching. Further, while it is my hunch that "non-selectivity" was intended by Noddings to indicate all students, I suggest that *all* of the teacher is also a crucial issue. Being there for children means freedom to be there as a whole person. How we construct ourselves as persons for our students is a purposeful act. Teachers who are comfortable with who they are are more able to "be there." Those who are preoccupied with life issues outside the classroom are less able to center on children and their needs. Noddings's construction of care as a metaphor for teaching has parallels in texts that predate the publication of *Caring*. One is Gilligan's (1982) research on care as an outcome of women's (separate) moral development.

WOMEN'S MORAL DEVELOPMENT AND CARING

Carol Gilligan's *In a Different Voice* (1982) provided an alternative to more traditional views of moral development. Women, Gilligan maintained, form their moral decisions on an ethic of care, which is grounded in their relationships with others and remains connected to others. These characteristics are presented by Gilligan in contrast to Kohlberg's (1981) stages of moral development. In studies that used only male participants, Kohlberg had established that justice and autonomy were the underlying tropes that resulted in a developmental, hierarchal model of moral reasoning. In response, Gilligan interacted with female participants to develop an alternative model, which was grounded in an ethic of care and reproductive of a developmental hierarchy (but one for females). In this model, morally based decisions that sought to resolve conflicts were based on relationships and connectedness, rather than a formal logic of fairness that Kohlberg proposed for justice-based decisions. A "care perspective" is an alternative that includes a network of connection, a web of relationships, and is sustained by a process of communication. Gilligan also includes affection, affiliation, and context as defining attributes in women's moral development.

Because of these potential differences between men and women, Gilligan (1982) suggested that "women [can] feel excluded from direct participation in society, [that] they see themselves as subject to a consensus or judgment made and enforced by the men on whose protection and support they depend" (p. 67). These perceptions can lead women to "a sense of vulnerability that impedes these women from taking a stand . . . [a] 'susceptibility' to adverse judgements by others which stems from their lack of power" (p. 66). Gilligan's analysis leads to the underlying effects of marginalizing women's meanings, lives, and language. Women's discourse becomes the unimportant, or incomprehensible, discourse of "the other" when viewed from a patriarchal perspective. This is not news, but it creates for me a strong case for the existence of a female underclass created by sociosexual oppression and maintained, at least in part, by the internalized response of these women (and men) who are oppressed. Gilligan goes on to characterize women's disenfranchisement as "drifting along and riding it out" (p. 143), creating the effect of an

> experience of women caught in opposition between selfishness and responsibility. Describing a life lived in response, guided by the perception of others' needs, they can see no way of exercising control without risking an assertion that seems selfish and hence normally dangerous. (p. 143)

Certain aspects of Gilligan's theory of care as morality appear to problematize Noddings's teaching-as-care model. While grounded in "morality-connected caring," Gilligan delineates the negative effects of such orientation. Women as carers are marginalized and vulnerable with respect to a male-centered reality of justice and individualism. As teachers, women are expected to, in Noddings's estimation, live "a life in response, guided by the perception of others' needs" (Gilligan, 1982, p. 143). Teachers in the primary grades (as well as other marginalized people) experience a paradox. Being connected to the lives of others through relationships, through caring, concomitantly requires the suppression of teachers' personal needs. According to Gilligan, women may perceive the promotion of their own individual needs to be inconsistent with an ethic of care. Yet, as teachers, they do isolate individuals as "others," or sites of caring. While Gilligan's construction of carers precludes self-ideation, it must paradoxically locate an individual as other in order to receive the self-care offered. Yet those same caregivers are also expected to control children, be accountable for curriculum, and manage commodities such as time, attention, permission, and toilet access. Gilligan contrasts this paradox of selfishness and self-neglect in contrast to the hierarchical and webbed social relationships that contextualize women's (including teachers in the primary grades) moral development. Webbed social structuring relies on an interconnectedness and a wish to be at the center of that connection, accompanied by a fear of being on the edge. Despite perceived differences in power distribution, things will be fair and everyone will be responded to and included. No one will be left out or hurt. It seems to me as if women's awareness of power hegemonies is a pervasive condition of life, and while differences in power may be acknowledged, they are not addressed, but set adrift.

Although careful to maintain that caring is not essentially feminine, Gilligan suggests that a morality of care tends to be realized socially as a female attribute. Conversely, a morality of justice and individualism tends to be male. In their moral development, children are able to solve moral dilemmas within both caring and justice frameworks. Gilligan (1987) suggests that children's ability to adopt multiple perspectives on morality means that *choosing* a moral standpoint is an element of the moral decision making we engage in. For me, this speaks against essentializing caring *or* justice as respectively female or male. However, socialization into expected gender roles reinforces notions of role-appropriate moral orientations. Caring is socially constructed as female, and teaching in the primary grades is equated with caring. Others, such as Nias (1989), have found similar relationships among women, teaching, and caring.

PRIMARY TEACHING AS CARING

In her description of teachers' views of their profession, Nias (1989) points up lives of paradox, ambiguity, and contradiction. However, it would be a misreading to suggest that such a characterization is necessarily negative. Rather, the descriptions are thickly layered and reflect the complexity of several realities that teachers simultaneously balance.

Part of the complexity stems from the beliefs teachers hold about themselves and their work. Nias (1989) suggests that "throughout their professional education and socialization, teachers are led to believe that they are capable of 'knowing' not just one child, but all the pupils in their care" (p. 15). Of course, to know even one other person is intense and complex work. To know 19 to 29 others, let alone the interactive effects of their knowing each other, seems a formidable task. Yet teaching in the primary grades is steeped in "knowing the individual students."

In my mind, teaching in the primary grades requires a selflessness that gives over one's personal agenda to the concerns of "others" (students). This seems not unlike Noddings's (1992) construct of teaching as caring. Many of Nias's teachers saw themselves as people with strong concern for others' welfare. About British primary teachers (roughly parallel with U.S. elementary grade levels, and subsequently distinguished from U.S. "primary grade teachers"), Nias (1989) says "they wanted (sometimes passionately) to improve the life-chances of children" (p. 32). Nias's choice of the words "sometimes passionately" is interesting here. First, it appears to me that Nias herself realized that this is a marked usage of words. A parenthetical statement, set off from syntactic flow, disrupts my attention and causes a focus on a passionate primary teacher. The construction seems to be an oxymoron. Yet, for the teachers in Nias's text, passion is located in children's welfare. Their fulfillment is found in their students' welfare. At this point, it seems to me that Nias can be read as making the subtle point that teachers are passionate about their students and, through omission in her text, perhaps little else.

Caring and the Self

In charting what Nias calls the substantial or core self, teachers breach the boundaries between the personal and the professional. Nias (1989) offers the following words from the primary teachers she interviewed:

> What's happening to you as a person can't be separated from what's happening to you as a teacher. (p. 182)

> Must establish a relationship with the pupils. (p. 186)

> It's not a question of education. It's a question of relationship. (p. 186)

> If teachers are going to be any good, they've got to have a really strong concept of what they are themselves. (p. 182)

Yet maintaining a "substantial self" in a social context that prizes giving to others is work that requires considerable attention from its participants. In fact, some teachers recognized the high cost and chose not to go along.

In speaking about a colleague, one teacher who was interviewed by Nias commented: "She put the children before everything else, even herself. . . . I'm not so committed to teaching that I'm prepared to risk my health for it" (p. 32). But apparently others are willing to risk their selves for their teaching. Nias summarizes with the following:

> To "feel like a teacher" is to feel you can be yourself in the classroom; to be yourself is to feel whole, to act naturally; to act naturally is to enter into a relationship with children, a relationship in which control makes possible the exercise of responsibility and the expression of concern; together these states enable you to "be yourself" in the classroom and therefore to "feel like a teacher" (p. 191).

The argument is intentionally circular and, therefore, highly resistant to critical examination. Believers continue to believe. But the equation doesn't balance when the construction of relationship is equal to control of others (students). Similarly, when the responsibility of caring is understood as a "must do" for individuals who are examining their own performances of teaching, acting naturally begins to sound rather prescriptive. Neither control of children nor mandates for teachers' caring behaviors are the same thing as acts of caring. These are oppositional constructs, or at least situationally circumscribed as such. The simultaneous consideration of control and caring is a rationalization for, in either direction, praxis that is incongruous. That is, controlling students in a caring context and expressing care for students in an authoritarian context are both instances of atypical, or negatively marked, behaviors that denote active (in the former example) and passive (in the latter example) manipulation. Walkerdine (1990) pinpoints the irrationality embedded in this mismatch of teachers' intentions and behaviors. According to Walkerdine, the production of rational students in classrooms requires an irrational displacement of teachers' lives. Second, the contrast of a teacher's orderly classroom with the potential for chaos outside the classroom walls points to a dramatic difference. These everyday conditions reconsidered effectively demonstrate that woman-as-teacher is given the opportunity to be the "container of irrationality" (p. 54). And as the fail-safe mechanism, or the shield for social dissonance, the teacher must sit out the half-lives of the fallout from the anger, frustration, and sublimation that accrue during these daily stealth assaults on reason.

Spender's (1986) descriptions of elementary teachers also suggest a theme of irrationality in her discussion of the paradox of care and control. Spender extends the earlier notions of primary teaching as care in more concrete examples:

> Elementary school teachers provide[d] total care of students. In addition to teaching lessons, teachers cleaned muddy boots, tied shoes, zipped zippers, cleaned up vomit, and other messes created by students who did not make it to the rest room on time, bandaged skinned knees, and monitored bathroom visits. (p. 171)

She also succinctly frames the nurture/discipline dichotomy. "Elementary school teachers could discipline students but also hug and kiss them, receive love notes and promises to 'be good'" (p 171). Yet she also cites teachers' responsibilities as curriculum and content purveyors.

While arguing for a professional niche for teachers of young children, it is important to look at the behavioral exemplars selected by Spender. The entire project of women's life histories as teachers is suffused with examples of caring as expected and devalued work. Most interesting in my read is that Spender presents these examples as objects for our veneration.

Nias (1989) appears to agree, at least as concerns the effects of the potentially dysfunctional roles occupied by British primary teachers:

> Yet, this sense of "wholeness" and fit between self and occupation is dearly bought . . . to "be" a teacher is to be relaxed and in control yet tired and under stress, to feel whole while being pulled apart, to be in love with one's work but daily talk of leaving it. (p. 191)

Woods (1987) concurs that the roles of primary teachers in Britain are axiomatically in conflict. On one hand, teachers are seen by the culture, and indeed they self-report, as having a strong desire for affectional relationships with their students and as encouraging a familial context for students. The teachers' own personal interests and enjoyment, their investment in a parental role, and their perceptions that students benefit from affectional relationships underpin their interpersonal relationships with students. On the other hand, teachers are also aware of their role as classroom manager, their responsibility to cover curriculum, and their contractual obligations to a school system. Woods (1987) argues for a "productive blend" (p. 143) based on teachers' personal attributes, training, and experience.

It seems to me that a "productive blend" of conflictual desire says little about the possible psychic costs of striking the balance. It also seems a falsely static resolution of something that defies a grasp, a fix, or a final resolution that frees the problem solver. Rather the "idea that teachers have *constantly* to strive for a balance between authority and friendliness" (Nias, 1989, p. 189; emphasis added) more fully describes primary grade teachers' movement within what can be seen as productive ambiguity. Teachers work this balancing act second to second in emerging interactions with individual students. It is a struggle of self-representation when the welfare of the other is the focus. It is simultaneously taking care of a self who is a person con-structing a "human-as-teacher" response to a first-grader's needs.

Care as Commitment

Another way Nias (1981) identifies primary teachers' work is through their reference to commitment. According to the British teachers she inter-viewed, commitment can also mean caring. Caring in turn is demonstrated by teachers when they teach in "inclusive" ways, or ways that involve the whole teacher and the teachers' whole lives. Commitment as caring renders the boundary between professional and private lives porous, and teachers interviewed valued the integration that permitted (and required) boundary crossing. In fact, Nias (1985) suggests that primary teachers in part choose their work because of their sense that they would be able to enact core values associated with caring—for students and for each other.

Once they are part of a primary teaching group, the teachers' values are sustained by connections with key reference groups. The teachers' con-tinuing discussions with their reference groups served to define themselves as well as the "reality" of the surrounding context. Those who had no reference groups, "that is, who had no one to whom they felt they could talk" (Nias, 1985, p. 107), came to deny their adults lives and often left teaching.

To cope, the primary teachers in Nias's (1985) extensive studies identify with reference groups. Adult reference groups are found both inside and outside the school. Inside, adult reference groups, such as grade-level teams, lunch groups, and committees, "confirmed goals and aspirations, kept them from leaving the school, supported them in innovation and retrenchment, deepened their satisfaction and fueled their discontents" (p. 112).

In contrast, outside reference groups (e.g., churches, rural clubs) al-lowed teachers to maintain their "substantial selves" but did not foster greater integration into the school social culture. Further, the more teachers identified with external reference groups, the less they were inclined to seek identification with the other teachers at their school sites. Finally, teachers who tended to identify exclusively with their students as reference groups were essentially isolated from professional relationships with colleagues. These teachers were also prone to leave the teaching profession.

Talking Care

Talk seems to be a critical element enabling the formation of individu-als' values and of shared values with their affiliated reference groups. Teach-ers make sense of their social circumstances in these ways. Yet talk itself was not seen as important by Nias's participants. In fact, Nias (1985) has suggested that, aside from reference groups, there was an "absence of opportunity or appetite for talk or discussion" (p. 115). Similar descriptions regarding teachers' lack of professional discourse or technical language have been offered by Lortie (1975) and Hargreaves (1991).

Teachers' "lack of professional discourse" is not a neutral description. Rather it entails some preunderstandings about what counts as professional language and an a priori value for "the technical." To attempt a different understanding of teachers' use of talk might lead to different conclusions about whether or not "they have it." Silin (1995) argues that teachers' use of vernacular language in preference to a learned (or technical) vocabulary may make them less susceptible to external controls. With its accompanying rules for enactment and use, a more "professional" language could be used against teachers to appropriate their work for the maintenance of patriarchy. With uniform definition, language becomes commodified into an object. External control of language as an object makes possible the control of object relations inside the profession that uses that language. Silin (1995) provocatively argues

> that it is women who most frequently bring children into language, who possess a primal verbal (biological) fertility that men cannot seem to forgive . . . the institutionalizing of language instruction can be read as central to the psychological movement through which men sought to heal this linguistic wound, by transforming ordinary language into the subject of hermetic discourse. (p. 153)

Subordinated relations, linguistic and otherwise, stabilize a patriarchal economy, which might be threatened by females' fertile capacities with interiorized and private language. Heilbrun's (1988) paradoxical argument concerning women's narratives applies here as well. Women's lives, argues Heilbrun, as they are portrayed in texts, are either written "flat" or written as men's lives. Because of narrative convention, and because of the representation of lives allowed women in texts, we have no means to portray lives that women actually live. Analogous to elementary school teachers' "nonprofessional" teacher talk, Heilbrun recommends that women create a separate discourse, that writers writing about and for women turn toward the center and write in newer, more self-serving ways. Yet, as with any essentialist arguments about marginalized identities, or language, or theories of moral development particularly for women, "different" can be read as "less than." So while some lament the lack of a technical vocabulary for teachers, Silin suggests that the lack of a specified or technical language may have helped teachers resist external controls for their work.

Silin's cautions are concerned with others' evaluation of our talk as it occurs among other adults. Our discourse with our children is yet another matter. The argument that primary teachers' choices of the linguistic frames and lexical items for child-directed talk do not constitute a "professional language" is logic that is, to say the least, irrational. We may well choose to speak to adults in more complex syntax or in words of several syllables. But devaluing language directed to children is axiomatically illogical. The children are our profession.

Primary reference groups result in and continuously maintain multiple realities within a school, including multiple linguistic frames. However, the use of multiple "dialects" or discourses can also cloud communication. Teachers apprehend a mistaken sense of having come to agreement over school purpose and philosophies, as well as practice. In fact, each may be connected only to selected reference groups and remain fairly distanced from others. According to Nias (1985), in short, primary "teachers neither wish nor are able to talk to one another" (p. 116). Further, creating an explicit and shared linguistic frame, or professional discourse might threaten the personal autonomy that Nias sees as the teachers' "substantial selves." Rather, sharing information within self-selected reference groups may allow elementary teachers some degree of personal autonomy within the larger social context of the school. Nias's conclusions regarding teachers' wishes not to talk with each other seem more plausible when viewed as referring to talk that is outside a reference group.

The perception that teachers do not interact can also be seen as a function of the ways that they teach. Galton, Simon, and Croll (1980) found that British primary teachers spend about 80% of their time interacting with their students. For 60% of the day, primary teachers worked with individual students. Relationships with individual students comprised the majority of primary teachers' days. This commitment to students leaves little time for talk with other adults.

SUMMARY

These looks into descriptions of the culture of primary teaching suggest care as an organizing construct. Caring about children as a teaching philosophy and caring for children as enactment of that philosophy are regular, valued, and ubiquitous in narratives, interviews, and descriptions of teaching in the primary grades.

Communicating extensively with children, especially in one-to-one situations, is a common feature of primary grade teaching. In contrast, in depictions that focus on teachers' lack of interaction with other adults, teaching is often characterized as a "loner occupation." Teachers' lack of a professional (technical) language, particularly among those in the primary grades, is often blamed on the teachers themselves. These contradictory and potentially ambiguous characteristics make teachers' talk a discourse frame that challenges both those who would learn it and those who would depict it.

These are the issues that confront all teachers in the primary grades. They are intractable. They are everyday things. For men who wish to teach in such an environment, the understanding of these issues can take some interesting twists and turns. The study that is described in the following chapter was undertaken to find out what teaching as caring might be like for men who chose to teach in the primary grades.

CHAPTER 3

Learning from Men Who Teach Young Children

It is difficult to determine when this inquiry into men teaching in the primary grades actually began. I had spent several years teaching in first, second, and third grades in Florida, Texas, and West Virginia. Even while I taught, I was wondering, like Agar (1980), "Who am I to do this work?" As the only male teacher in some schools and as one of only a few in others, my performance as "teacher" was noticeable, at least in relief. But to what degree do I make that difference a way of understanding myself as a teacher? Alternatively, why bother to see myself as a male in a context in which my making such a distinction may be irrelevant?

The paradoxes presented by males teaching in caring contexts that were discussed in the previous two chapters prompted me to investigate several male teachers' perspectives on teaching in the primary grades. In this chapter, I present a description of the study, include its guiding questions, examine my involvement in the study, describe the data collection and analyses, and provide a brief introduction to the participants. Since the researcher is the primary instrument in qualitative inquiry (Bogdan & Biklen, 1992), it is also productive to describe my role as a researcher and the impact I had on the study.

MY LEARNING ABOUT TEACHING

My first year of teaching was with a difficult group of sixth-graders who had been removed from the other sixth grades and banished from the building, with me, to an off-site special education room. We were a disgruntled bunch. One of my mentors that year, Beth, patiently listened, gave me confidence in myself, showed me learning centers, and watched as my students ripped them to shreds. I also had some good years. Danny Williams's mom adopted me, became my room mother, and helped me see students as children, as people. That same year, but with a confusingly different agenda, Susan's mom, Betty, sent me an engraved ID bracelet, cologne, and underwear for my

25

Christmas gift "from Susan." I spent some time confused by these different constructions of who others thought I was. I didn't have a clue who I was.

My new wife was a teacher. Her father was a teacher. I became a teacher. I had married at age 19 in my sophomore year of college; after graduating in December of my senior year, I was teaching full time in January. In the 22 years that followed, I would leave elementary classrooms for college teaching, leave the Midwest for the South, leave my wife to find a new life on my own. At 36 years old, I "came out" as gay, learned to "date," and settled down with my partner, Richard.

The central questions about who am I when I teach, and then when I'm not teaching, have always been there, but more recently, I have focused on the question: What happens when teachers who are male teach in domains that are thought to be female? To further complicate the question: What does it mean if the men are gay? These layers of identity formation and conflict lend weight to the questions that guide this study.

The issues surrounding men who teach young children are often personal ones. Since 1973, when I began teaching in the elementary grades, rumors, jokes, gossip, and warnings about teachers, sex, and students have been constant. In teachers' lunchrooms, conjoining the topics of teaching and sex can halt any other discussion. In the community, such loose discussion can mean the end of a teaching career. These are life-changing issues, significant to every teacher, but nobody is talking (out loud). Instead, we all tacitly conform to "touch hysteria." Johnson (1995, 1997) suggests that our current fears surrounding the meaning of touch in teaching is eliminating all touch as inapproapriate. If he is correct in his analysis of our current obsession with a "no-touch policy," we may soon be teaching young children from behind glass enclosures or in germ-proof bubbles.

These issues resurfaced in my current job of mentoring preservice elementary teachers in an elementary department. Over and over, I heard "Why are there so few men in elementary teacher education?"—giving me a chance to attempt to understand my own "touch hysteria." The questions I pursued in this project came from my experiences as a male teaching in the primary grades.

WHY SO FEW? A RESEARCH QUESTION

The initial purpose of this study was to examine "Why so few?" from the perspectives of the men who chose to teach in primary grades. I was interested in their perceptions about the factors that might be dissuading other men from becoming teachers of young children. As the study progressed, the interactions among participants narrowed the focus of our work to an examination of gender roles in primary education. Such changes in focus are part of the richness of qualitative inquiry. The following sections describe the selection of the participants, the interview process, the writing processes of the participants, and the focus groups.

Selecting Participants

I started by formally requesting permission to conduct this study from three contiguous counties on the west-central coast of Florida. The three countywide school districts were very different. One was a sparsely populated, rural county; another was a coastal resort and residential area; and the third, the nation's twelfth largest school district, was comprised of both urban and rural areas. More than 2.5 million people lived in the general area of the three counties. In the three counties, there were 215 elementary schools with more than 9,000 teachers, 656 of whom, or roughly 7%, were males. Within the group of male teachers, 121 men taught in K–3 classrooms.

Each district approved the study after a committee review and, at my request, provided a printout of all male elementary classroom teachers. Each of these men was mailed a copy of an initial demographic survey with a cover letter. Of the 121 surveys mailed, 78 were returned. From the returned surveys, I selected potential participants for interviews, based on a balance among age, years of experience, and grade level of teaching. For age, I established a continuum of participants between 23 years and 71 years of age. Years of experience in the teaching profession ranged from first-year teachers to 25-year veterans. I also stratified the respondents into grades K, 1, 2, 3. I excluded teachers who were not currently in K–3 classrooms or who were teaching special subjects, such as music or physical education. Based on my experiences, this latter group tends to have different teacher/ student relationships than do classroom teachers. In contrast to teachers of special subjects, who see children for abbreviated periods of time, classroom teachers have continuing, day-long contact with their students. The focus of teachers of special subjects may also be restricted to certain content issues. I thought that their experiences would constitute a very different set of understandings about teaching.

In a second purposeful sampling technique (Goetz & LeCompte, 1992), I asked two gay male teachers who taught in the primary grades of the three counties to participate in the study. As "out" gay males, their perspectives on gender issues in teaching were ones I wanted to include in the current study. These two participants introduced to me to other gay men who were teachers in the primary grades in the three counties. Two of the participants who had originally joined the study group by responding to the survey identified themselves as gay. I ended up including information from only three of the four gay men because the fourth was unwilling to be interviewed on tape and did not want his information used in the study. Of the three gay informants, one chose to withdraw from the study after three interviews, but he consented to my use of that data. As my role in the study shifted from researcher to participant, I became a fourth gay participant.

In addition to the gay male teachers, there were five heterosexual male teachers in the study group. In total, besides myself, there were eight active participants in the study. Of those eight, seven remained in the study to completion.

The Interview Process

I began the interview process with a phone call to set up a first meeting. I asked for the participants' permission to audiotape. The initial interviews took place in teachers' classrooms, in their homes, in my office, and in restaurants. The interviews were guided by my requests to "tell me about your teaching experiences." Follow-up questions focused on aspects of shared experiences that related to gender issues.

During the interviews, I listened and did not take notes. As soon after the interview as possible, I listened to and transcribed the tapes, adding my memories as bracketed commentary. I also kept notes of my own thoughts as I listened to the tapes and made references to readings that had some relationship to the topics discussed.

I analyzed each participant's audiotapes and transcripts for themes that emerged from repeated readings of transcripts and repeated listening to the tapes. Themes became important with repetition and explicitness. Once identified, these emergent themes became a rubric to examine individual cases for patterns. These examinations with reflexive use of thematic categories form an emic description of that one teacher. I also looked for a match between issues I had previously been concerned with and predominant characteristics exhibited by participants.

The first and second interviews took place 4 to 6 weeks apart. I was able to have a third (and even fourth) interview with some participants. In all cases, review and analysis of the previous interview(s) guided the subsequent one(s). The interviews were conducted in an open, unstructured way. We often shared experiences as primary teachers. Occasionally, I prompted with questions from the first (or other previous) interview(s). I offered audiotapes of interviews to informants, but none chose to listen to them.

Participant Writing

During the second interview, I invited each of the participants to write something about their teaching lives. With each participant, I talked through some ideas and themes that seemed to characterize our interview together.

In all cases, I tried to ensure that the choice of topics and the stories told about them remained the selection of the writers.

We also discussed an approach for reading and responding to each others' writing. After talking with each of the men individually, I mailed them a summary letter inviting them to write and mail me their writing. All participants except one mailed me a draft copy of a story, a remembrance, or a theory. I then mailed each participant duplicates of the writings for the whole group. Participants agreed to respond to each others' writing and to consider revising their own writing based on group feedback. A second mailing with revised drafts was followed by a focus group meeting.

The Focus Group

In the focus group we hoped to talk about the second drafts, share some ideas about teaching, and get to know each other better. I was also looking for confirmation or amplification of the underlying issues that I perceived in the interviews. Themes that emerged during the focus group reflected the diverse topics that had emerged in individual interviews and in personal writings. These results, which I summarized in a follow-up letter to the participants, included the following topics:

> *Pedophilia.* It had always been a lurking suspicion; now we are talking about it.
> *Sexuality.* This is automatically projected onto male teachers; we shouldn't touch students.
> *Discipline.* Male teachers are expected to be accomplished disciplinarians.
> *Second careers.* For men who come to elementary education from previous careers, it may mean greater security.
> *Teaching focus.* Men may teach more to content, curriculum; women may focus on relationships.

As I listened to the tape of the focus group, I was surprised at how circular our discussion had been. Each of the themes we identified was also used to explain the occurrence of the other issues in the list of themes. For example, the reason male teachers should not touch children is because we are seen sexually. As a researcher, the confirmation of the grounded theory (Glaser & Strauss, 1967) that was generated was reassuring. Yet, as a teacher in the primary grades, I was frustrated by the lack of resolution. My emotional response was part of the rationale for the analysis in Part III.

INTRODUCING THE PARTICIPANTS

Brief descriptions of the eight men who participated in the study follow. The men who chose to write are further described in their own writing in the chapters in Part II.

Paul[1] was 38 years of age; after a successful decade in business, he was enrolled in a master's program that would also certify him as an elementary classroom teacher. It was his painful recognition of sexism in elementary education majors that propels his story, which follows in Chapter 4.

Steve was teaching first grade in the suburbs. Gender equity was a major issue for him. He reveals several interesting ways of gently, persistently testing what he understands as permissible behaviors in teaching that enforce how one should behave as a teacher and how those rules were often based on gender expectations. His views are explained in Chapter 5.

Ken had been teaching kindergarten for 17 years. He was outspoken about his beliefs about children, how education best addresses those beliefs, and his role as "the one" responsible for keeping it all in balance. Yet his writing in Chapter 6 is about his life that is unknown at school. He is gay, and he writes movingly about the effects of grieving on his teaching as his partner sickened and then died of AIDS.

A second-grade teacher, Gregg was moving to first grade the next year. He was excited about the move but subdued in sharing his news. His careful, quiet style permeated our interviews and his talk with children. After holding several teaching positions at the primary level, he was going to have a chance to "find out what it's really like down here," a warning issued him by a female colleague who was critical of male teachers in the primary grades. But changes were not new to Gregg, as his writing tells us in Chapter 7.

Cal was teaching third grade when we talked. He had been teaching for 17 years. At the time of the interviews, he was pursuing a move to kindergarten but was proceeding with caution. His major concern was with a lack of match between his curriculum philosophy and that of his co-workers. His writing in Chapter 8 makes a cogent point about differences between activity-based curricula and language-mediated curricula.

Evan was a character. It is a role he cultivated. In our talks, in his text, he tested tolerance. His approach in this writing was to test readers' reactions. He said he used his "difference" as a way to be independent in his teaching. At age 71, he was comfortable with his designation. In Chapter 9, Evan and I enter into an imaginary conversation about his and others' teaching.

---

[1]All names used in this book are pseudonyms.

Van was finishing his first year as a teacher after years as a foreman in a boilermaking factory. He described his approach to teaching as caring in self-aware, matter-of-fact language. Both he and his wife made career changes in midlife and spent this, their first year teaching, together in the same elementary school. Van's writing does not appear as a chapter, but I drew from our interviews in my chapters of analysis.

Fred had just finished his first year of teaching after several years working in geriatric care, followed by undergraduate teacher education as a 30-year-old. His perspective on this first year was unique. His current relationship to teaching had become so painful that he found it difficult to talk about and chose not to write about it. Data from our interviews is included in the chapters in Part III.

Each of Chapters 4 through 8 was written by the indicated author, with the assistance of all the other participants and myself in a writers' workshop format. One of our last formal meetings together was held to share what were then the final copies of the participants' stories.

PART II

Inside Views from Male Primary Teachers

CHAPTER 4

It's Still Sexism

Paul, Undergraduate Elementary Education Major

I know something about Rosa Parks now, something I never knew before: I know how she felt, that hot day in the back of the bus.

My male friends ask me what it is like, living out your fantasies—or, at least the adolescent fantasy of being surrounded on all sides by members of the opposite sex. I am one of the few men in most of my classes; often, I am the only one. When men ask me about this, a certain glaze appears in their eyes, you can almost see them mentally salivating at the prospects of this imbalance in ratio. Some leer and ask me if it is like being a kid in a candy factory. I smile at their ignorance of its realities and tell them it is not anything like they might think. Then, if time permits, I tell them a story about an experience I had recently, which has given me much pause for thought.

This summer, I took a methods course that was focused on teaching social studies in elementary school. Although I didn't know the students in the class, as they were from another teaching team, I didn't think this would present too much of a problem—since I really didn't know the members of my own team all that well, either. I was excited about this course, because I have always loved social studies. It presents the opportunity to bring history to life, make it relevant to current issues. The professor clearly had a great deal of teaching experience and passion for the issues presented in the coursework. I looked forward to learning about techniques that could be used to teach this subject more effectively. Professor Andrew's philosophy is essentially that the classroom ought to serve as a model and laboratory for the social values we teach, and that we, as teachers, are very important models in that process.

Early in the semester, we began to discuss values education and the techniques that can be used to teach it. As a means of illustrating the point, we read passages from the Bill of Rights, the Magna Carta, the Mayflower Compact, and the Constitution, discussing the meaning, intent, and origins of these documents. The discussion then shifted to the creation of our own classroom constitution. This activity was intended to help children develop social skills such as building consensus and brainstorming, as well as to make more real the challenges posed by the creation of these documents. "Respect Others" was given the consensus priority in our classroom constitution; this was to be the guiding principle for our own class for the summer. This contract was written on posterboard and taped to the wall, as a reminder—just as we might remind our own students someday.

The last activity for this unit on creating a classroom constitution was called "Space Shuttle." In it we broke up into small groups to discuss the following problem: You and your group are on a spaceship, headed for an uninhabited, earth-like planet, where you are going to settle. Before you land, however, you must resolve several questions: Who will govern you? How will you select them? What rules will you have? What are you most concerned about?

In our group, Deborah looked right at me and, in a perfectly serious tone of voice, unsmiling, delivered this pronouncement: "Women should rule."

Heads nodded around the group at the apparent wisdom of this dictum, and a quick glance at their faces revealed nothing to indicate that they were anything but serious. A chorus of "yeahs" and "uh-huhs" followed.

Looking back on this, I see with perfect clarity that I must have taken this as some kind of challenge, although at the time I didn't have enough insight to realize this. In any event, I rose to the bait, little realizing, as the hungry young trout chasing the mayfly lure, the disaster I was inviting.

"So, let me get this straight—selecting a political or social position on the basis of gender characteristics is going to be OK in our new world?" I asked. Another thing I realized, in hindsight, was that I didn't even look at the other group members—I was so surprised by Deborah's seeming intellectual insensitivity to the issues we had just finished discussing. I also felt shut out by the agreement of the other group members.

"No, I'm saying that men have made a mess of things here, and they shouldn't be given a chance to mess up the next planet."

Heads swiveled, as if at a tennis match.

"I don't dispute that men haven't exactly covered themselves in glory, but is this a gender problem, or a human problem?" I questioned, thinking of such notorious female rulers as Catherine the Great and some of the English queens, wondering if it was even worth bringing up.

"No, its definitely a male problem"; this was delivered flatly, not inviting further discussion.

"But what about the principles we've been discussing, of equal opportunity for all persons, respect for all?" I pressed, now looking around our circle for some support. In the end, we managed to agree that a representative democracy would be acceptable, with equal roles for both genders. We spent so much time on that question that we weren't able to get to the others. The tone and process of the discussion gave me much concern, though, about how the others might have been treated.

Deborah hasn't spoken a single word to me since that day.

At the conclusion of the activity, each group briefly presented their scenarios. The first group leader got up and described a world in which the men would wear thongs, be musclebound and tan, and feed the women grapes, amidst much laughter and sideline discussion in the room. The second group leader envisioned men bought and sold as slaves; in the third, men would be confined to camps, allowed out only for the purposes of procreation.

As I watched and listened, I was struck by the momentum of the sentiment expressed, how the energy level and volume of sound increased in the room, at the sharp tone of the deliveries. I put on my "good sport" face, the one with the half-smile and nondirectional eyes, and rode out the storm. Much later, I realized that I was shutting down emotionally, although I didn't know it at the time. I think this is what Rosa Parks must have done, every time she got on the bus with the "Niggers Ride in Back" signs, or heard the slurs on her race and gender as a part of her daily life.

I slipped out of class, confused, disturbed, but unable to identify the source of my disquiet. I just vaguely sensed, in the way that we sometimes sense we've forgotten something but we can't think what it is, that something wrong had just happened. In the hours that passed on that Thursday afternoon, I found myself growing angry and puzzled by my mood. That evening, at home, as I worked on my journal, I suddenly realized what had happened: I had been on the receiving end of blatant sexism, the kind of treatment that could have resulted in lawsuits and headlines if the genders of all the participants were reversed. I found myself thinking, "Well, OK, I guess I'm just supposed to take this—after all, I'm sure that they've been the target of this kind of treatment often enough," as if rationalizing it would take the pain and inherent wrongness of it away. But I was unable to delude myself in this fashion, because I started to think about who we are, and what we're training to do, and what all this might mean. *Then* I became really angry!

What I've learned to do over the years when this happens is to ask myself, What are you afraid of about this situation? So, I began to explore the levels of it. First, I noted my concern about my own inability to recognize what was happening as it happened, and how I would need to improve in this area if I was to be a decent classroom teacher. Second, I recognized my very deep concern about the apparent hostility toward men, which I suspected might be embedded in these scenarios, and how that set of values might be inadvertently transmitted to children in the classroom. Third, I suddenly critiqued my own construct of women as exclusively "sensitive, nurturing persons." That was only part of the picture. Finally, I confronted what else I was afraid of: My conscience would not permit me to ignore this situation. I would have to talk about this, and I realized that in so doing, I risked alienating people who would be my colleagues not only in school but also in the workplace—people whose support I would need in order to be effective.

The following Tuesday, after our next class meeting, I approached Professor Andrews about my understanding of our group dynamics and how it might be addressed. To her credit, she was chagrined at what had happened. She had gotten caught up in the surface humor and momentum of the event but later sensed that something might have slipped by her. This provided me with some insight into the dynamics between educators and their students on interpretive issues, such as this instance of sexism. I wondered how a male professor might have responded to this, or whether the students would have presented the same scenarios in a male professor's class. I agreed to withhold comment for a period of time, until the opportunity presented itself later in the semester's course work. In the meantime, I spoke with my language arts professor (a male), who encouraged me to write about it, and I discussed it with some of my female peers who weren't in that class. Finally, I approached one of my colleagues in the social studies class to get a reaction. "Hey, did you have the same reaction to class that I did?" I asked. She had, and told me of her own misgivings. We talked about whether I could, or should, confront this, and she encouraged me to speak out. I waited, even though I didn't like sitting on it. I thought about how destructive this kind of avoidance due to social/professional considerations of practicality must have been, must be, for all kinds of persons, particularly women. I wondered if this accounted for the hostility I sensed being acted out.

Finally, the moment to speak out came. During a discussion of current events, Professor Andrews went around the room, questioning students on whether they were biased in any way. To their credit, most of them agreed that they had some prejudices—but not where it came to issues of gender. I raised my hand and spoke for a few minutes about my feelings, my experience, my concerns about the events on that fateful day. Professor Andrews asked for comments after I was done.

"Hey, we were just kidding." Maybe, but if it was so funny, why didn't you construct similar scenarios about black people—there was one of them in our class, too, but you didn't pick on her.

"Well, OK, but haven't you ever done the same thing?" I wondered if two wrongs of this type canceled each other out.

"What's the big deal?" You mean you don't know?

"Well, you don't have to do anything to get a job, while we all have to bust our butts!" As if I don't! Do you work full time? Has your career choice cost you your marriage? Do you struggle to find time for visitation with your beloved child in between all this?

After class, one person came up to me to apologize.

Since that day, I have been subjected to various hostilities, including alienation from group work on a semester term project, cutting comments in and out of class, glares and cold shoulders in the hall. I seriously considered dropping the class, but I decided that this would be giving in, legitimizing their views by my absence. I wouldn't give them the satisfaction, I decided—all the while telling myself: Here you are, thinking in terms of "us" and "them." This process of dehumanization takes on a life of its own if you're not vigilant.

I have seriously considered what all this means—for our schools, for my career. I have questioned, and continue to question, whether I am making the right choice to be in this program. Then I remember the kids and why I decided to do this: because it counts. You have to believe in what you're doing or else you can't be effective. That's why I walked away from a successful business career 3 years ago. I couldn't go back to it now, even if I wanted to. That's why I eat peanut better sandwiches—a lot. Because it counts.

I think Rosa Parks knew that, too. You do things in life because they count. I think she could no longer live with the injustice, or with herself for tacitly agreeing to it by her silence. One day, she decided that she, by her actions, would stand up for what she believed, no matter the consequences.

We cannot have a healthy society, or happiness in our own lives, if we continue to model the dynamics of sexism, whatever form it may take. What we do, who we are, the emotional baggage we carry—it comes with us into the classroom. This is what kids learn from, most of all. So, I will watch myself, and ask others to help me, deal with these issues. And I will speak out if I have to. I couldn't look Rosa in the eye if I didn't.

It counts.

CHAPTER 5

Men in Primary Education

Steve, First-Grade Teacher

I did not have a man as a teacher until I was in the fifth grade. I really liked him. He was fun and it was like having a second father. I remember he took a few of us to see a baseball game each grading period. Maybe I paid attention more that year because he was a man. Whatever it was, I did well in school that year. In seventh grade I had another male teacher. In all, I had seven male teachers through the twelveth grade.

In college, I was the only male in the majority of my professional education courses. I had the chance to study children and women at the same time. When I say "study women" I mean I observed their behavior in situations and how they interacted with children. I feel this also helped to develop the caring and nurturing side I have today. In most cases I was friends with the majority of my classmates. They all seemed to accept me and the fact that I was going to be an elementary teacher. Yet I felt that I had to "prove" myself and do the very best that I could. I concentrated and did all the projects with the understanding that I had everything riding on this one chance to show I was able to do the same things as a woman and sometimes better when it came to educating. It was at this time that I found I did not appreciate the fact that some professors used me as a role model in class. "I like the way that Steve did his project." I felt that this would cause a few of my classmates to dislike me. I wanted to be liked by all and not disliked because I was a focus in my education classes.

In all of my teaching positions, a factor that I had to deal with was hugging students. When I first started working at a day-care center, I was nervous because of the hugs. I grew up in a family that was not very touchy and huggy. I had to develop the hugging while at college. I watched the females in my class and tried similar techniques when I dealt with the children, who are, after all, the point of all this. Children do not see a man or woman hugging them. Nor do they do think it strange for a man to hug or show affection. Adults are the ones who put stipulations on the hugs or touching. "Why did he hug my child?" "How did he touch you?" Questions such as these are more often asked about male teachers than female teachers. It is much easier for a woman to show affection toward a child than it is for a man. Men and women may be hugging children for the same reasons—to show we care or to make them feel better—but other people may believe that a male teacher has some kind of underlying motive for a hug or gentle touch. I hug my students on a daily basis. We have an understanding in a way that I usually get all of my hugs when we are traveling in the hallways. When we line up for computers, music, physical education, or art, the children will give me a hug. I return the hug with a gentle sideways squeeze. Also at dismissal time, the children who feel like hugging me can do so. I never request a hug. It is always their voluntary act. I had a few students over the years who never gave me a hug, and that was fine. There were a few who only gave them to me as we came back from vacation breaks. Hugs probably go along with how I communicate with the children. I am as honest and open as I can be.

In addition to difference in hugging, voices also make men and women different as teachers. Male teachers may have what some consider harsher voices than female teachers. I am always aware of this when I communicate with the students. I am usually standing somewhere in the room or sitting on the floor while we do some of our lessons. I try to keep my voice moderate, although I can become very loud if I need to. I have only raised my voice on two occasions—and then apologized for doing so. I feel that yelling does not solve the immediate problem. I will keep a steady voice or often lower my voice so the ones who are listening will benefit. I talk to those not listening in private. When not listening is part of a larger behavior problem, I give the appropriate color card, which is part of a discipline plan I use.

Like most teachers, I have also developed nonverbal communication. Facial expressions and hand cues help to inform the children that we are changing the lesson or that someone needs to refocus his or her attention. I also communicate with them through writing. They write in their journals daily, and I always respond with a positive comment or question. I also believe that male teachers have to communicate differently with female teachers than other females would.

Most of my communication with my colleagues is about school or ideas for a special theme. We use certain teacher language that a nonteacher might not understand. The teachers I have worked with seemed not to be bothered by my being a male. I'm sure most of them did not discuss personal female problems with me as they would have had I been another female. In turn, I did not discuss personal male problems. This may hold true in most work locations, not just the teaching field. We discuss general topics at lunch or at our meetings. I believe that many of the normal female conversations were modified or changed so I could be included. At one point, I chose not to eat in the lunchroom because of a personal conflict with another teacher. A female colleague said that it was because they are always talking about women things. From my perspective, that was not the reason, at least not the main reason.

Being a minority has some disadvantages. First, a male in primary education is more closely watched as to what he wears. Women teachers can wear just about any type of clothing and usually it looks nice. According to school policy, women can wear shorts, providing they also wear stockings under them. In fact, women can wear shorts with or without pantyhose and get away with it. Presumably, it would be sexism or harassment to ask a woman, "Where are your pantyhose?" In contrast, I have worked with principals who have insisted that the men wear neckties. Wearing neckties presents few problems for me, but it seems like requiring ties on men is asking for clothing that is different from what I normally wear. I am very active in the classroom and become very warm doing most of these activities. I wear short-sleeved dress shirts and dress pants. I would love to wear shorts but was told that doing so might result in a negative mark on my yearly evaluation under "dresses appropriately for work." I was also told that if I wore pantyhose with my shorts, it would be OK. This was said in jest, of course. Women appear to have more freedom in the way they can dress for teaching than do men. If a man wears accessories, he may be questioned about why he is doing such a thing. In the future I would like to develop a line of clothing for male teachers—something that is masculine but eye-catching to the students and teachers. I would like to see a lot of primary colors. So be looking for those clothes—I am working on it!

Another disadvantage is the close, watchful eye a man is subjected to. Is he performing correctly in the classroom? Is he developing the curriculum in the proper way? I don't mind when people come to my room or visit unannounced, but some people do. I love to have people in the room. I have nothing to hide. As I am a very creative teacher, I love to find a challenging way to have fun and learn at the same time. I often take risks and enjoy doing so. I took a risk when I went into elementary education. I could have chosen any other profession and done well in it. Instead I chose this profession.

I am able to compliment myself and feel comfortable with it. I just don't like it when others use me or my teaching to tell others how it should be done. I had a principal once who would say: "You should be more like Mr. Norris." "Talk to Mr. Norris." "He knows about that." "See how Mr. Norris did that." I told her that I felt uneasy about her praising me in this way, especially since, invariably, it would be when a group of people or the entire faculty were present. I just wanted to be liked for myself and not because the principal said I was good. I worried that people might reject me if I was talked about in this way.

Another disadvantage is disciplining. I don't enjoy being the "heavy." Some teachers will send their problem students to my room for time-out. I have been told to my face that I would be better for them because I am a man. What if I was not there? Whom would the child be sent to then? I don't mind helping out a colleague with a discipline problem, but I have my own to deal with. I have also been told that I was the selected teacher for a certain child because *he* needs a male teacher. I have not yet been told that I have been selected because *she* needs a male teacher. I still wonder about the reasoning behind these decisions.

What really annoys me is when I make decorations, cupcakes, cookies, party favors, or refreshments for a classroom or faculty function and a co-worker asks "Did your wife make those?" I almost go insane. I used to just politely say, "No, I did." Now I am bolder and say, "I took care of these matters before I was married! Now that I am married, and my wife enjoys baking and making food trays, we create together."

I do the majority of the cooking and baking for the classroom because I enjoy it and I take pride in my work. I like to see the wonderful smiles on the children's faces when I bring in something related to a current theme or topic we are discussing in class. I not only create decorations and make food for the classroom, I also do T-shirts as well. It was something I thought of and implemented: birthday shirts for the children to wear on their day. The shirts are the school colors and simply say, "Hooray, It's My Birthday!" I do a lot of T-shirts for myself as well. I keep them simple and related to topics and themes during the school year.

There is also an advantage to being a male teacher. The children notice you more. A colleague and I were walking through the hallway when we passed another class. Almost all of the children in the class said, "Hi, Mr. Norris!" None of them had said a word to the teacher I was walking with. She pointed that out to me.

I believe there are more men out there who would really like to teach the primary grades but are unsure or disillusioned about how they would be perceived by peers and society. All I can say to them is that you have to work through the disadvantages and overlook the stigmas that have been placed on this profession for men. In the next 2 to 5 years, I would like to see at least one male teacher in grades K–3 for each building. I would like to become a specialist in early childhood development and help other males to be effective and enjoy the art of teaching. I would also like to see support groups for male teachers established in each county if not statewide.

CHAPTER 6

Caring for Others While Teaching

Ken, Kindergarten Teacher

The summer of 1987 was the first summer in my career that I didn't have to teach. The larger tax return I received as a new homeowner enabled me to cover my summer expenses. My lover Gary and I began the summer by celebrating our second anniversary. Our celebration was short-lived.

Friends had begun to comment on Gary's health. He had lost weight and lacked the energy he used to have. His job was physically demanding, and I attributed his tiredness to the summer heat.

The HIV antibody test had just been approved, and he and I went for anonymous testing. The procedure was to draw the blood and wait 2 weeks for the results. During that period, Gary developed chronic diarrhea and was hospitalized. Blood testing at the hospital revealed that he had HIV antibodies, and he was diagnosed with what was then called Aids-Related Conditions, or ARC. He remained in the hospital for about 10 days.

While he was hospitalized, I returned to the anonymous test site to learn that I had tested negative. One of my first questions to the nurse/counselor there was whether I could carry any illnesses to the primary-age children whom I taught. She assured me that this was not possible, nor could I carry childhood diseases home.

Gary was working light duty when the school year resumed. Shortly after Labor Day, I caught a cold, which happens to me about the beginning of every school year. Gary soon developed a similar cold, but it got worse, and he was hospitalized with *pneumocystis carinii* pneumonia (PCP). As a result of that diagnosis, he was now considered to have full blown AIDS.

He remained in the hospital for the better part of a month. I continued to teach during the day and spent the evenings and weekends at the hospital. At that time, the hospital did not allow a "significant other" (my designation on Gary's chart) to stay overnight in the patient's room. He took a

44

disability retirement from his employer and received Social Security disability.

I was very fortunate at work. My classroom aide had a daughter, who was my age, and a gay son. He and I socialized, so my aide had known that I was gay prior to our working together. About the time that Gary got sick, her husband developed a chronic illness that led to his disability. She and I were able to commiserate about hospitals, doctors, and illness and to support one another.

With the support of my classroom aide, I carried out planning for class and interactions with the children and with colleagues reasonably well. Working with young children, I am so busy that thinking about my personal problems, or any other issues not directly concerned with the youngsters in front of my eyes, is very unlikely. In some ways, submerging myself in my work with the kids was therapeutic for me.

I wanted to be fully informed about Gary's condition. He allowed me to accompany him on visits to the doctor. But it was often difficult to schedule his appointments with doctors after the schoolday ended at 3:00 P.M. On one occasion, I had scheduled an appointment on a faculty meeting day and asked the principal for permission to leave early and miss the meeting. At that time the mother of a member of the office staff was in critical condition, and the staff member had missed a lot of work. The principal repeatedly asked me what was wrong with Gary, but I refused to tell her that it was AIDS. I explained that it was something that I could not transmit to the children and that he had had pneumonia so many times in his life (which was true) that he was in a very weak state.

The principal then advised me that if her parents were to take ill, there would be nothing that she could do for them and she would have to remain at work. If they died, she would then take one day off to attend the funeral. I replied that Gary's family was unable to care for him, so the burden had fallen to me. I was granted permission to miss that meeting. At that time my principal was willing to conjure her own parents' demise in order to convince me that leaving school before the end of the day was a problem. Though I was circumspect about my use of AIDS as a label, I feel certain that her resistance to my leave was as much related to her fears of AIDS manifestation as it was my absence. In subsequent years, the principal's attitude about missing work for another's illness has become more lenient. I think some of this lenience, perhaps even compassion, stems from her experiences with Gary's death and my part in it.

In early December of 1987, I came home from work to find a message from Gary's mother on the answering machine. They had been Christmas shopping when he had fainted, and he was taken to the emergency room. He needed a transfusion, the second in three weeks. AZT, the only medication available at that time, was depleting his red blood cells. The doctor advised Gary to discontinue the AZT and "get his affairs in order."

From what I can recall of that year, my teaching of kindergartners was not affected by Gary's illness, except for having to leave early for occasional doctors' appointments. A friend worked near where Gary and I lived, and she was occasionally able to drive Gary to doctors' offices, where I would pick him up after school.

I took off the summer of 1988 to spend time with him. He developed a blurring of vision in one eye that was diagnosed as cyclomeglavirus (CMV). He was referred to a nearby medical school, where the ophthalmologist referred him to an immunologist who put him on an experimental drug to treat the CMV.

For the first week of taking this drug, Gary went to a local teaching hospital, where he could be monitored. This hospital had a special unit, modeled on one in San Francisco, that was exclusively for people with HIV and AIDS. The staff was either gay or gay-friendly, and they recognized Gary and myself as a couple. At Gary's request, I spent one night sleeping on the sofa in his room. Otherwise, I would spend most of the day and evening with him.

School resumed that fall, and once again, I caught my beginning-of-school cold. Once again, Gary developed PCP and was hospitalized, this time in the teaching hospital. I spent every evening and the entire weekend in his room, leaving on Sunday nights to go home to get ready for school. Gary was hospitalized for about a month this time. I arranged for his sister, who was visiting from out of town, to bring him home, so I wouldn't have to take a day off from work. She agreed.

Following that hospitalization, Gary lacked energy. I would leave the cereal box and bowl out on the counter for him and a sandwich in the refrigerator, so that he could eat while I was at work. Again, I was so busy with the kids that I didn't have much time to dwell on Gary's condition. He was able to dress, toilet, and feed himself independently at this time.

After Valentine's Day 1989, his condition deteriorated. I was attending a workshop at a school near our home and was able to go home for lunch. He told me that the doctor's office had called, wanting to see him in the office, about some blood work that had been done several days earlier. I wanted to take him right then, but he insisted that I wait until I was finished at the workshop that afternoon.

The doctor determined that he needed to be hospitalized, based on his weakness and the results of the blood counts. (Two weeks before, Gary had been treated for dehydration in the doctor's office.) Gary went in an ambulance, and I followed in my car to the teaching hospital.

I got back into my old routine of spending the evening at the hospital, leaving around 10:30 P.M. to return home so I could get up to teach the following day. Gary was admitted on Thursday, and I spent the weekend at the hospital, as I had done in the past.

That Monday morning, I had a phone call at school from Gary's doctor, advising me that Gary's death was imminent and to get to the hospital as soon as possible. I explained this to the office, and as soon as a substitute arrived, I raced home, packed a bag, and went to the hospital.

Gary's condition continued to deteriorate, and for the next 10 days I lived at the hospital, leaving only for 2-hour stretches at a time. I checked in with my aide to make sure that things were going well in my classroom. At one point I asked Gary's mother to stay with him at the hospital, so I could go to school after hours and write the following week's lesson plans.

On Tuesday of the second week of my stay at the hospital, I had a message on the answering machine to call a co-worker. She said that she had heard that the principal had called her secretary into her office and asked how many days I had taken for Gary's illness (our contract allows absence for the illness of a member of our household) and how many sick days I had remaining (which at that time was in excess of 30). She purportedly went on to tell the secretary that once word got out about Gary's illness, no one would want to use the same restroom or water fountain that I had used. It has never been clear to me whether the principal was trying to anticipate others' reactions to Gary's illness or whether she was using others' hypothesized reactions as a way to express her own beliefs. I guess it doesn't matter now. And even then, the secretary responded that I had worked a long time at this school and was well liked by the faculty, and if the principal caused problems for me, she would probably have to take on most of the faculty. My co-worker reminded me that our annual evaluations were due at the district office and that I needed to get back to work so that I wouldn't be poorly evaluated in the area of attendance.

I returned to school the following day, looking pale and drawn. I had advised my aide to let me know if I acted too stressed in front of the children, but she never felt the need to mention it or to suggest that I needed to leave the room to compose myself. I resumed my routine of working with the children during the day and spending the evenings at the hospital.

That Friday, in a moment of lucidity, Gary asked me to stay overnight in his room. Initially I agreed, but feeling very tired, I then declined, stating I would get a better rest at home. I left the hospital around midnight. About 2:30 Saturday morning, the hospital called to tell me that Gary had died. His mother and I made funeral arrangements that afternoon. The following day, five staff members from my school paid a sympathy call to me at home, bringing food.

On Monday, I returned to school. I took Tuesday afternoon and all of

Wednesday off for the visitation and funeral. My principal sent a large floral arrangement to the funeral home, as did my team. The other two teachers on my team visited at the funeral home that evening. Private funeral services were held on Wednesday in Gary's father's home town, 50 miles away.

When I returned to school following the funeral, the principal apologized for not coming to the funeral home as she had been ill. She expressed concern for my finances with Gary gone and said that if I needed money, she would be happy to lend it to me. Again, I have mixed feelings about her motives. I am grateful remembering her generosity.

Gary and I liked the book *The Velveteen Rabbit.* In separate conversations with the pastor, each of us had requested the same passage to be read at his memorial without realizing the other had done so as well. Toward the end of the school year, the children saw the video of the book. The only time I cried (my eyes briefly watered) at school was when the video got to "our part." Before showing the movie, I had explained to the children that someone very close to me in my family had been sick and had died, and they seemed to take it in stride, sharing their stories of grandparents or pets they had lost. The children continued to keep me so busy that I couldn't dwell on my problems. On occasions when I felt sad, one student in particular would wind up doing something silly that would cause me to shake off my maudlin mood.

Throughout Gary's illness I was teaching the Positive Action program that teaches one to turn negative thoughts into positive thoughts. This program helped me to maintain my calm throughout his illness and death.

CHAPTER 7

Working Within Gender

Gregg, Second-Grade Teacher

My earliest recollections of gender bias go back to when I first started college. I was attending a teachers college in upstate New York in the late 1960s. Out of a graduating class of about 800 students, 600 were in elementary education, but only 20 of them were male. I was one of the 20.

I was very much encouraged to go into the elementary education program, and I always felt I received extra nurturing by advisers and counselors to stay in the program. I even remember one particular professor, of whom it was said that she wouldn't give anything below a B to a man in her class, as long as the work was completed. From my current perspective, such a statement would trouble me because of its inherent sexism. But at the time, I felt simultaneously special and marginal.

My family was very supportive of my decision to go into education. I come from a blue-collar family, and I think there was some pride on their part in having the first son graduate from a 4-year college with a degree rather than a trade. I don't mean this in a derogatory way. I just feel that a large part of my parents support, emotional and financial, was given so that I could achieve something more than they had, could break the mold that they had been in. It is a complex realization that they were proud that I would not be like them, at least in my work.

I also grew up in an era when there was still great respect for someone in the teaching profession. Whenever I was asked, "What are you going to college for?" I would reply, "To be a teacher." There would always be a smile and some reply like "Wonderful." Today the question is still asked, but the reply of "to be a teacher" is replaced by "to be a professional educator in the field of literacy" or something or other. We have lost the self-respect that was evident on our simple, direct use of "teacher."

One of my first realizations that men in elementary education were not the norm came when I said I was going into education and the assumption was that I would be teaching high school chemistry or algebra. When I said, "No, elementary school," the reply was, "Oh. P E" When it was finally understood that I wanted to teach reading to small children, the reply was, "Oh?"

Thirty years later I no longer get that questionable understanding when I say I teach elementary school. What I am asked, however, is why I am still in the classroom. Why haven't I gone on to administration? This is the easiest question to answer. Working in the classroom, especially in the primary grades, is one of the most satisfying, enjoyable, and challenging experiences I could have. There is an unexplainable satisfaction that comes when you watch a child learn or when you know, as is true in many cases, that you are giving something that a particular child may not get at home, know that you are helping to shape the future of a child. There is an unbelievable feeling of gratification that comes over you when you look into a child's face and see that you have reached that child. It may be the smile you see after you give a compliment, or a wide-eyed look when you are reading or telling a story, or that "oh yeah" when something is understood, or just the hug that the child wants to give you. These are the feelings that make the day very worthwhile and motivate you to return the next day to try to reach the ones you weren't able to reach the day before.

My first 4 years of teaching were in the intermediate grades. When I look back on those teaching experiences and at myself, I feel that my naiveté and overexuberance led to an early burnout. I left teaching after those first 4 years, not to return until 12 years later.

During my first try at teaching, I had the feeling I could solve all the problems, make every child a successful learner, and win the admiration of my colleagues. Everything had to be done to show others that I had the model classroom. It was true that children were enjoying themselves and learning at the same time, and the classroom looked creative and inventive. However, I also remember a sense of anxiety about not being ready or able to control the many different parts of teaching. I think some of the pressure I felt had to do with standing out as a male. Being one of two men teaching in the intermediate grades (there were 25 women), I always felt I had to show not only that I could be successful in this female-dominated institution but also that I could be better. I never felt that way while I was preparing to be a teacher, but once I was in my first classroom I was aware that there were some doubters out there about a male entering "their world." There were always heads popping in the door to see what was going on and questions about what I was doing. With a few exceptions, none of this was done with encouragement.

When I look back at those first years and remember how I dealt with the parents, I am amused compared to how I feel today. Having just graduated from college, I found that most of my students' parents were around the same age as my parents. Having been brought up to respect adults, I found it difficult to sit at a conference and discuss a child's problems with and offer solutions to someone I would want to go to for some of the answers. And yet I was the one person supposedly trained to give those answers.

By the end of those first 4 years, I began to realize that I couldn't help every student, I didn't have the answers to all their problems, and I couldn't respond to all the queries of their parents. I felt that I wasn't doing the job that I had set out to do. What I didn't realize at the time, but do know today, was that I was probably doing a good job but had unreasonable expectations for myself. My youth, inexperience, and idealism were in the way.

I left teaching and went into business for the next 12 years. I can still remember when that first September came around after I left teaching. There was a big void in my life, and I wondered whether I had made the right choice. I missed the children.

Outside of education, I made more money and also grew up. I wonder now what kind of person would have emerged from an incubation as an elementary teacher if I had stuck it out in the classroom. I know I have brought much into my teaching from my years in business. While in business I often thought about going back to college to renew my teaching certificate or getting another degree in education, but the time never seemed right. Then, while visiting friends in Florida who worked in a school system, I discussed my interest in getting back into education. Before I left after my 2-week visit, I had two job offers to teach in the elementary grades. I went home, packed up, and had that piece of chalk ready for the next September.

When I reentered the classroom after 12 years, I noticed many changes. There were more men. I was teaching third grade, and there were 4 other male teachers on a staff of 25. One of these men was a first-grade teacher, and that fact surprised me. I had always been interested in teaching younger children but had thought it improbable. I had never encountered a man teaching first grade. I also noticed that the children had changed a great deal over 10 years. My third-graders looked the same as I remembered them, but their attitudes and outlooks were entirely different. Parents also looked different—I was older then they were! There also seemed to be a different attitude in the school. Twelve years later there were more specialists and the support staff was larger. Teachers were more involved in decision making.

After 4 years I relocated to another school district in Florida. When I interviewed, I found that men were still at a premium in the elementary schools. If you were a black or Hispanic male, you were worth your weight in gold.

After 3 years of teaching in my new assignment in fourth grade, there was finally an opening in second grade, which I had been waiting for. All my teaching experience had been in grades 3–6. For a number of years I wanted to work in the earlier primary grades. I was the first male second-grade teacher the school had ever had. I was really excited about the change. I felt I had some strong teaching qualities that were important in the early primary grades and that there was also a growing need for male role models because of the many changes in the family structure.

When it became known I was going to second grade, I was met with some interesting questions: Are you sure you're going to like it? Do you really know what you're getting yourself into? I remembered the male teacher who taught first grade when I came back to teaching. Although he was a father of two sons, a soccer coach, and a great first-grade teacher, he hadn't been accepted by his female counterparts. Men in elementary education were no longer considered an oddity as long as they were not in the primary grades. Teaching in the primary grades was still a female domain.

I have taught for 2 years in second grade, and this coming year I'll be teaching first grade. When the principal announced that I would be filling a first-grade opening, more little light bulbs began to light up in my head. From the reactions of some of my colleagues, I realize that there are still many professionals who do not think I am appropriate for first-grade teaching simply because I am male. They seem to have preconceived notions about who is appropriate for which job without any regard to abilities. I found that there are some women, who have been in the profession for many years, who are very intimidated by changes. I was questioned about whether I was ready to wipe noses, tie shoes, and fix buttons and zippers. And the best was, "He'll really find out what hard work is now, when he comes to first grade!"

I have found that parents generally like having men in the elementary system—but not always for the reasons I choose to be there. There is this notion that a male teacher will straighten out that child who is a discipline problem. A large number of parents have said to me that their son or daughter has been a problem and a male teacher is what the child needs. I guess what they are saying is that there aren't any female teachers who have good classroom or discipline techniques.

Early on in my career I felt intimidated by parents, even when they were supportive, because of my age and lack of experience. Today I look at parents differently: They are part of the partnership. If they will work with you and support you, it's wonderful for the child. Too often though, teachers must work without direct parental support. I have come to a point in my life and career that I feel secure and competent enough to tell parents directly about the needs I perceive for their child, both in my classroom and in their home. However, many parents aren't ready to listen.

Since I have reentered teaching, I do things with the same determination and sense of pride that I had when I first started, but I have a feeling of confidence and self-assurance that I didn't have before. I think part of this has come with age and maturity, but I feel that some of it has also come from being away from the profession for a few years and working in the business world. It is very easy to fall into a rut when you do the same thing the same way for so many years. There are many teachers who have done that. This is one reason that they feel intimidated by any sort of change.

Since I have been teaching in the primary grades, I've become more aware of myself and changes I have had to make. After teaching a number of years in the intermediate grades, there was always concern, sometimes expressed, sometimes not, about touching and being too close to the students. It became a practice not to be alone in a classroom with a student, and no "hands on" was allowed for any reason.

At different points I always sit back and ask myself: How are things going, and am I getting the results that I have set out to get? One day it occurred to me, after watching another second-grade class with a female teacher, that the children's rapport with her was significantly different from my students' relationships with me. Her class was always grouped around her, hugging, holding her hand, sharing secrets. My class didn't have that closeness. We weren't a family; we were a class. I was the person in charge. I felt a nurturing atmosphere was important for children of this age. I had to break some of those rules that said a male teacher couldn't touch, he had to be a strong disciplinarian, he had to be a strong father figure. I knew that if I was going to be a good male role model for these children, at an age where it might have some influence, then I had to resensitize myself. I didn't make drastic changes in my teaching, but I felt secure enough about knowing children's needs and about my own masculinity to make some changes. Being sensitive to a child's needs—whether it means giving a hug or holding a hand—is a quality that is a must for a primary teacher. This is something that I had to become aware of and comfortable with, and the hugs back and hand-holding have been the payback.

Unfortunately, there is still a stigma attached to being a primary grade teacher. Elementary schools are still female-oriented—from the way faculty rooms are decorated to the "girl-talk" atmosphere of faculty meetings. I still hear the announcements: "Boys and girls, your teacher has a notice for you to take home. *She* will. . . . "

CHAPTER 8

Certification, Language, and Learning

Cal, Third-Grade Teacher

"Cal Crippen, a teacher? Never in a hundred years. An elementary teacher? Never in a thousand years. A kindergarten teacher? Never in a million years." It's difficult to believe that 23 exciting years of elementary teaching have already passed and that retirement is close at hand. How did it happen? Becoming a teacher was an unusual combination of circumstances: love of history, economic necessity, and pure luck.

HOW I CAME TO TEACHING

It all started in southern Greece, where I had been residing for 3 carefree years. Living in Greece put me in the cradle of Western civilization, surrounded by ancient ruins, the statues, and the theaters that were part of my family's and all of our cultural origins. It became apparent to me that most of the accomplishments that we enjoy today were already thought out in Greece about 2,500 years ago.

An urgent letter from Mom stating that Dad was to undergo a serious operation sent me home. I knew that this would be a turning point in my life, and within several days I was with my parents in Florida. At age 34 it was about time to take on some responsibility—and, in addition, wedding plans were on the horizon. What a contrast with my idyll in Greece!

Now, I faced finding a job. I wanted to teach history, but when I visited the local school personnel office, I learned that a B.S. in economics was not acceptable. Certification in education was required.

The next move was to get a degree in education. Here is where luck came into play. After several fruitless trips to the university, one of the deans suggested that I see Dr. Willis, who might have something of interest to me. Disappointment was my initial reaction when Dr. Willis explained that he was looking for candidates to enter a K–3 culturally disadvantaged program, but subsequently he convinced me that possessing a love for history and teaching small children were not incompatible. He convinced me that the program would lead to a master's level degree, with a fellowship provided along the way.

The following 18 months of academic coursework and, more important, daily classroom observations (one grade each quarter) quickly taught me the importance of teaching young children. I also learned that I enjoyed the open minds of the children. I learned that a well-rounded child is one balanced in cognitive, affective, and psychomotor skills. After interning in a Head Start class, I realized that I was interested in teaching kindergarten. What impressed me was the curriculum, which was based on teachers' manipulation of students' concrete experiences.

This time when I returned to the county personnel office, I held the certificate whose lack had formerly kept me from teaching. The personnel staff was surprised to see me again, and within a few days I received an assignment to teach kindergarten at Bell Elementary. "Never in a million years???" Never say never.

Should it take such unusual events—an ill father, a love of history, and Dr. Willis—to guide a man into teaching at the elementary level? It seems obvious that a more organized way to steer young men into education needs to be instigated at all levels of the profession. Think of all the money that is spent convincing our youth to enlist for 3 to 6 years in the military. With the end of the Cold War, it is obvious where the greater need lies. Financial aid would also attract young men who could not otherwise afford a college education. Some might become fine primary teachers. I feel that once someone is actually involved with the educational process they begin to realize the need and importance of teaching and it becomes apparent how they can contribute and fit in. It certainly happened to me.

My family and I often returned to Greece to relax and visit friends and relatives. In 1984, our children, all of elementary age, stayed in Kalamata and attended Public School #7. Most of the teachers were men and highly regarded in Greek society.

The lack of male primary teachers could be one of the contributing factors to our tragically high crime rate. Consider the boy raised by his mother, attending elementary school with a succession of nurturing female teachers during his formative years. We are now reaping the results. A childhood lost is an adult lost.

Never have I worked harder or longer than during those 5 years at Bell Elementary. I endured double sessions without an aide or air conditioning. There was never a dull moment or a chance to catch my breath. I had been attempting to transfer closer to home to avoid the long daily drive (34 miles, round trip). Finally the opportunity to teach in my own community came, but at a great cost, I would be teaching third grade. Little did I know that is where I would remain for 14 years.

SOME THINKING ABOUT TEACHERS' GENDER AND CURRICULUM

The greater part of the teaching day is in the classroom, with the students, and the gender difference between teachers does not surface. It is at meetings or workshops where it becomes apparent. At our school the ratio of women to men is 18 to 2, but I have been at workshops where the ratio is much higher, like 100 to 2. I quickly realized that the elementary school is a matriarchal fortress and that being careful in word and actions would be critical to my survival. At times this has been very difficult, and on several occasions I wish I hadn't expressed my viewpoint, because the tone of my voice revealed my frustration mixed with anger.

Once a male professor stated that reading was primarily a psychomotor skill. This caused turmoil in the class of almost all female teachers because it downplayed language arts. He had a terrific time explaining that reading was a medium for cognition, not one of knowledge itself. I have always felt that the language arts program was overemphasized at the elementary level. Perhaps that is why I prefer teaching kindergarten—because children are learning through manipulation rather then being hung on the *word*. When curriculum is hung on the word, then any learning is mediated by students' abilities with language. While manipulating language is analogous to manipulating objects, it is much more abstract when done within the parameters of enforced accuracy. Retention may be improved where children have opportunities for concrete experiences embedded in curricula that are realistic from students' perspectives.

There is a tendency for women to be more comfortable with language arts activities. Because of the sheer number of female teachers in elementary education, they control the curriculum and the emphasis has been in language arts. Things seem to be changing. The reading specialist has a new title of "curriculum specialist." Also there is an attempt to link or coordinate the language arts with math, science, and social studies. It seems that integrating subject areas has led us to project-centered learning that at least has the potential for real activity-based learning. A bias against activity in classrooms and toward language mediation of activity will continue to place young boys at risk in their own classrooms.

I am not sure that there is a solution to gender-based differences in curriculum preferences, and maybe there can't be one. However, as long as women teach most of the primary grade students, and these early grades are construed as literacy crucibles, then children will be impressed into literacy.

CHAPTER 9

What's Wrong with Teaching and What I Do About It: A Conversation with Reflections

Evan, Third-Grade Teacher
Jim, Interviewer

Evan and I first met in a restaurant. The location was my choice, but everything else that evening was under Evan's control. Immediately, I felt trapped and defensive as he looked at me over the top edge of his glasses. His white goatee and white, brushed-back hair framed the challenge in his face. I wanted out of this situation.

Since this first meeting with Evan, I have come to realize that much of his manner is posture, or performance. His exaggerated use of superlatives, his use of abusive language, his apparent sexist devaluing of female teachers—all are certainly oppressive to me, offensive as well. Yet, as I continued to listening to Evan, there emerged a sense of quality and ownership about his teaching and his students that is worth sharing. My involvement in Evan's chapter is to sort out the relevant arguments and present them, beginning with Evan's view of teaching:

When the word *teacher* comes to [my] mind I think, naturally, of elementary school. That is where teaching happens. And when I started in the school business, I had two children in the local public schools. Yet, in my preparation to teach, I found that schools of education do not provide the necessary foundation for a person wanting to teach children. Methods courses have nothing to do with producing thinking, problem-solving, creative adults. The minimum requirement for admission to a classroom should be an undergraduate degree in some discipline or liberal arts, and a further degree in methods.

A teacher must bring competence to a classroom. In Norway, before entering the profession, one must first spend a full year in a real job, in the real world—not in a family business. Most of our teachers have never had to earn their living at some sort of work. Few of them have background in music, art, or literature. What can such intellectual paupers bring to any elementary classroom?

At this point, I am reminded of the Holmes Group certification initiatives. I waited for Evan to make the comparison, but he didn't do so. After the following question, he mentions coming to teaching after several decades in business.

JIM: If you are so convinced that teachers lack competence, then why did you choose to be one?

EVAN: I chose elementary school because that is where formal learning begins. It's where the action is. I spent my first year in sixth grade and was not satisfied with the literacy of my kids. The next year I was a fifth-grade teacher, and still not satisfied with the quality of learning my kids brought to the classroom. I worked my way down to fourth and to third and *rarely* came across a child who had been required to write a sentence, no less a paragraph or composition. Ditto sheets and workbooks, with their required filling in of blanks, was, and largely *still is*, what goes on in classrooms purporting to teach reading/language arts.

I agree with Evan on the lack of value in most ditto and workbook exercises, and realize that his direct, confrontational style is starting to gain some context. I begin to recognize that this verbal assault I'm sitting through at dinner is some kind of test. If I want to know him, to learn about his teaching, I will have to also learn to depersonalize his "colorful language" and vitriolic condescension toward his colleagues.

EVAN: I wanted to catch the kids early enough to get them to use words with style and humor. I wanted them to acquire ownership of a thesaurus of their own. Sylvia Ashton-Warner and Herb Kohl taught me that the teaching of reading is, in truth, largely a matter of creating writing . . . children must speak first, then transpose their words to paper . . . and when they write, they are learning to read in a highly personal way. What my children talk about, we write out together on a large chart. Then we practice reading, together and individually, from the group chart. My kids' scores on standardized tests prove I'm right. We have consistently beaten the grade level by at least a year in reading. But what is more important, my kids begin to understand and value the currency of language. In experience charting, the whole is greater than the sum of its parts.

The teaching of language mechanics, requiring book reports, instruction in grammar—all of them are destructive. There is a systematic pattern of research that questions teaching grammar. Yet teachers whose own language is something less than standard American English persist in deadening children's interest in the richest, most beautiful language on earth!

JIM: Once again, you are finding the fault inside the teachers. What do they say about you?

EVAN: Other teachers think I'm interesting. They compliment me on programs my kids have created. They know that I don't use basal readers or any other texts. I'm old enough to be their father. So I'm an ancient eccentric, interesting, slightly kooky, highly effective, *but* peculiar. I do everything wrong. The teachers have drinks with me and laugh at my stories. But I'm "not quite right."

JIM: What about the differences that exist because you are male and they are females?

EVAN: There are differences, and some of them may be related to gender. I find that the classroom is just about the most exciting place in the world for someone who takes joy in learning and seeing kids change. Most of the male types I have met in elementary education were drones—are drones—and they rise to the top of the educational system.

Evan connects me with the unexamined assumption that we, males in elementary education, are in training for a principalship. I am left to wonder why Evan and I have not followed this path. In contrast to rising through the ranks of education, Evan recommends transferring competence from outside education into the classroom. I'm also made aware that, for Evan, maleness is inextricably linked to competence, job performance, and accomplishments:

The person with a background of success is aware of his capabilities. He has proven competence. He has dealt with real people in real situations. Most "school" is not real. It's all pretend and role playing. I've met very few adults at any level in schools who could keep a real job of work in the real world, dealing with grown-ups and real problems requiring solutions. What, in the classroom, seems to be risky behavior is simply an adult's solution to a problem in his unique way—because he has been in the neighborhood before. And with age comes a maturity born of experience that makes problem solving a tolerable effort. One is assertive, not dependent. But most teachers are dependent and need guidance and supervision. They're big children in the classroom—actually no more worldly wise than their small charges.

The gauntlet is thrown down once again. I see the explicitly drawn sides of Evan's argument. I can choose to follow his reasoning—to remember the problematic teachers with whom I've worked, the problematic teachers I have been. We could all be better I think, with travel, with reading, reflection. Presumably, more knowledge would have made me a better second-grade teacher in Star City, West Virginia. In many ways, I was a big child then. I knew little about this region in the Appalachians, and even less about myself in a new marriage, job, and state. But I don't deserve to be treated so harshly for who I remember being.

I can resist Evan's reasoning and disagree about how ineffectual he would think I was as a second-grade teacher. His argument seems elitist, individualist, and typically masculinist, inside a nurturing social context. I think of the "lone wolf" metaphor. And even with my judgment of him, Evan is ready with a sarcastic parry:

Teachers aren't supposed to become ruffled, upset, annoyed, or angry. They must at all times be calm, placid, serene, bland, robotic. When I'm angry, the kids know it. When I'm pleased or distressed, they know that, too! Teachers should be people with emotions who are able to show them and control them—and understand them. My kids are, indeed, kids. I want no interference from anyone. Nobody cares more about them than I do. Nobody knows better how to present learning opportunities than I do. Nobody cares more than I do. And nobody cares based on experience and intelligence and the willingness to keep reading, keep inquiring, keep willing to grow and *change* like I do.

The lone wolf prowls his classroom turf:

I've been verbally scolded and marked down on evaluations for not showing proper respect for children. I was told that in elementary school [a teacher] must never reject anything the child does. "Everything has merit." Baloney! Some stuff is worthless. Kids will get by if you allow them to, and they'll excel if you scorn less than their best effort. I refuse to accept less than what I know to expect from each child. And I may be gruff about it. Kids are not little Marines, but the Marines learn to do the best they can do and take pride only in their best. My classroom is a boot camp where most kids ultimately come to value themselves and recognize their uniqueness and abilities. I don't coddle

them. They get hugs and kisses (on the forehead) on a regular basis—
and they get hollered at when I am not disposed to accept mediocrity
from an able learner.

I see individualism and quality conflated with authority to yield an educational context that Nietzsche would be proud of. But Evan has even more
surprises. The same model that seems so authoritarian when describing his
own practice seems very child-centered when he talks about his teaching
desire and his students:

Today I finished the last day of my 28th year in the elementary school
classroom. I have 8 weeks in Britain and Europe ahead. I have spent . . .
every summer feeding my eyes, ears, mind in foreign countries. The
year that passed was a delight—kids grew, kids changed. The summer
ahead is another kind of pleasure. And when August comes I'll be de-
lighted to be back in the classroom, trying to find new ways to cause
children to learn to think, to try, to keep on trying until they read,
write, and cipher with satisfaction and a feeling of pleasure. The
"Thank God it's Friday" crowd has always been annoyed when I respond with, "Yes, just think, it's almost Monday!"

The kids are the key to my program. They are the *reason* and the
method and the *content* of the curriculum in my classroom. What's curriculum? It's what happens in the classroom. How do the kids become
the key? My entire approach to learning is to make the child the feature, the star, the center of what transpires. How? By having learning
occur in the affective domain. First, there are no texts, no reading
groups, no book reports. Reading is developed by incorporating different types of writing. Before a child is ready to write he/she must be
given ample and rich opportunities for speaking, for expressing personal opinions and feelings. Glasser opened me to getting the child to
open his mind and mouth to express doubts, fears, and longings.

One strategy is the weekly guest in the classroom. Over the years
I have assembled an all-star cast of performers and have added to the
program as often as I encounter an interesting adult. The local arts
council has provided invaluable help. Every week some grown-up is in
the room to interact with my kids. Representatives of local and state
government, business professionals, and performers from the arts visit.
The butcher, the baker, the candlestick maker, sword swallower, snake
charmer, psychiatrist, mayor—you name him or her. I'll go after him or
her to persuade him/her to play with my kids. Some are flops. Many
become regular visitors. The assistant attorney general for the state of
Florida had been a visitor every year for decades. The kids hear about

the functions of the members of a court. In the process one or more of the kids makes a connection to the story of Goldilocks (or something similar). Before long we have a mock trial of Goldilocks, with kids taking the parts of all the storybook characters and officers of the court. Is this a way to learn social studies? Is this a way to develop listening and speaking skills? Is this a way to develop language and the use of language with style and purpose? I suggest that it is.

Depending on the particular nature of the visitor's program, I sometimes ask the children to write about what has transpired. They have become involved. They were participants in role playing and questioning, they have had a good time. They laughed, they reacted, they enjoyed. "OK—now write about who came in, what you saw and heard and did." They become willing to push a pencil to squeeze out words "from your head, to your hand, to your pencil . . . " They write about what they know, what they have done, what has touched their lives. That's one way to generate writing, reading, spelling, and language.

Every year in elementary school is much like every other. The same subjects are taught at the same time. For the same duration, with the same kind of materials, texts, tests, and board work in which all children are expected to do the same thing, in the same way, to get the same right answer. My students learn the meaning of unique very quickly. Some years ago Ruthann, a tow-headed, three-freckled, buck-toothed charmer, was in my fourth-grade class. Her baby sister who was in second grade came by every afternoon when it was time to go home. On Halloween day, baby sister held up the pumpkin she had made out of a brown paper sack and said to me, "See, Mr. Mitchell. See my pumpkin." And I said, "Yes, it's lovely! Is it like all the other pumpkins in your class?" To which she responded, "Yes!" And I said, "Well, you made it *right*, didn't you?" And she joyfully said, "Yes." Ruthann, my student, growled at her sister, dripping venom—"*You ain't unique!*" I am, my classroom is, my curriculum is, my kids are unique—and after 28 years I am, if anything, more excited and fascinated by the process, and the persons in the process, than ever before! The narrow confines of the county-prescribed, -proscribed curriculum call to mind Coleridge's lines about the mule on a short tether in a field of luxuriant grass: "and much I fear me, he lives like thee half famished in a land of luxury." There is no tether in my curriculum!

PART III

Reframing Primary Teaching from Three Perspectives

CHAPTER 10

Caring: A Problematic Model for Primary Grade Teaching

Primary grade teaching and caring behavior are nearly synonomous in our culture. Teachers of young children are automatically assumed to care about and provide care for their students. This chapter neither disputes nor devalues such beliefs. Rather, the purpose of the chapter is to reconceptualize how the intent to care affects teachers' work; to reconsider the relationship of caring to gender; and to consider how caring is deployed as teaching behavior.

TEACHING IN CARING CONTEXTS

Teaching in the primary grades can be seen as caring, and caring is often construed in our culture as women's work. Nevertheless, when the men who were interviewed in this study of men's teaching in the primary grades talked about their work, they spoke about their belief that caring for others is consistent with how they see their work.

Caring as a Way of Being a Person

An attitude of care is something that goes beyond the classroom walls for the male primary teachers. Steve had had several nonschool teaching experiences and several other service-oriented jobs before beginning his teaching in the primary grades. He had worked in preschools and in food service. Van talked about his desire to be "involved in children's lives, to make a difference for them." Fred, one of the participants who chose not to write for the project, came to his first year of teaching after a previous job of providing care for the elderly. Directly stated, teachers need to be skilled at relationships. There seemed to be a consensus among these male primary teachers that knowledge of children's emotional lives was a professional domain and that involvement in those lives was a desirable, even a required, aspect of teaching in the primary grades. And while these men were able to provide that kind of relationship, this ability was something they usually had learned or acquired over time.

As he related in one of our interviews, Gregg remembered his first experiences in teaching as unsatisfying, disconnected, and lonely. Other men frequently have such experiences as beginning teachers, but Gregg's understandings about it are revealing. He mentioned not getting the response from his young students that other primary school teachers received from their students. Gregg clarified his notion of response as including children's running up to other teachers, whose attentiveness signaled to him an emotional connection. As he observed his colleagues, he began to notice which of his own behaviors were keeping his students at a distance, both psychologically and physically. He decided to make himself more open to receiving his students' affection and to respond to their needs for his affection. He built up his affective teaching self by watching his colleagues interact with children. These observations became Gregg's lessons in caring.

Caring as Touch

As he told me this story, Gregg talked about hugs and touch in unproblematic ways. He had learned that young children need affection, acceptance, and warmth from their teachers. He had observed how others created opportunities for these conditions, and he proceeded to copy them. Likewise, Steve saw his female colleagues as his role models for teaching as caring. However, he had learned the "strategies of caring" earlier in his life.

> I did a lot of observing of peers in college about hugging. The girls always gave a hug, and guys, if they did give a hug, it was like [makes small pats on his back] real standoffish. I did a lot of watching at first. Even in the early childhood lab, I did a lot of observing. . . . I would watch them first and then try to. . . . It felt awkward at first. I didn't do any mess-ups or anything embarrassing, and then I did a few hugs and pats. (Interview, 3/11)[1]

Steve's language choices are revealing. First of all, the fact that hugging was our topic of conversation is significant. As an act of caring, hugging and touch are risky behaviors for men who work with children. Even the discussion of Steve's hugs as a unique occurrence exemplifies the risk of such behavior. That Steve so clearly remembers acquiring the skill of hugging

---

1. Interviews are identified with the month and day on which they occurred.

also supports this contention. Hugging and touch are integrated parts of a constellation of caring for primary grade teachers. Yet Steve's description of successive approximations, or even desensitization to his discomfort with hugging, offers a very different picture. Presumably, Steve was uncomfortable with hugging and had to learn to suppress his discomfort to accommodate the children's needs for hugs. His, as well as other men's, decision to teach in women's ways is a difficult choice, one that require abandoning preconceived notions of caring and learning.

Steve's phrasing (e.g., "did a few hugs") also reveals the compartmentalization of care as "a bag of teaching skills," as does the "add-a-skill" strategy he used to assemble his approach. Later, I will examine the construction of touching as a marked teaching behavior. At this point, however, it is interesting to note that "hugs" as caring behavior are seen as an object, something to get used to, something to "get over." This perspective is quite different from one that doesn't objectify hugging, gestures, or touch. Rather, these natural expressions of care are part of the relationship and the context.

Caring in Contexts

Caring is also reflected in the character of the teachers' classrooms. In Steve's first-grade class, a caring context provides options and activities within structured routines. He comments:

> I have a busy room. The principal brings people to my room. "Here's a man teaching first grade. He lets his students know what is expected. They move through an interesting day. And his room looks like the teacher down the hall." It's like passing some kind of test. (Interview, 4/2)

The social context of the school includes caring relationships with other adults. Here there is a respect, or a professional attitude, toward the work of others that communicates care. Gregg reasoned about the different styles or types of caring as follows: "With kids, teachers work with them, caring for them." The other reality of caring that he mentioned was involved the schoolwide relationships with other adults, which is typified by caring about other teachers or caring about children or teachers with other teachers. Gregg sees these as separate realities—"management and work with the kids."

Caring about children with other adults makes the children "objects" of care. So when teachers share their concerns with other teachers or with the principal about their students, the talk can objectify the students into a problem, a behavior, or a type. Professional caring—that is, teaching in the primary grades—implies a double role. Talking with others about our caring is to care about, or to be distanced from, the caring itself (Tronto, 1993). Caring as a professional endeavor means that teachers provide caring (caring for others) while simultaneously monitoring that they are providing care (caring about). This double role contrasts sharply with giving and receiving care inside a family, where caring roles are not so sharply differentiated.

One way to categorize teachers' caring endeavors is to consider face-to-face interactions as caring for, and other behaviors related to that interaction as caring about. For example, advocating on behalf of a student at a staff meeting, making a bulletin board, or discussing a child's problems with a colleague are a few of the acts of caring *about* children mentioned by the male primary teachers. Tying shoes, monitoring recess, or talking with a student about a pet turtle are acts of caring *for* children that were mentioned.

Whether a teacher is caring for or about children, the perspective of teaching as care has profound effects on men who provide it. There was a shared belief among the male primary teachers that this work with children was special and had transformative powers on teachers as human beings. As Steve put it: "In primary education, you become some[one] other than your person on the street. But it doesn't stop when we leave the classroom. It transforms people in good ways" (Interview, 3/11). Yet transformation, Steve was careful to point out, is not without its costs. His claim that he is involved as a whole person in a teaching mission is similar to descriptions of elementary teaching culture by Nias (1989), Noddings (1984, 1989, 1992), and Spender (1986). Steve knows he "is possessed" and monitors the emergence of his teaching self in inappropriate settings.

> I try not to act like my peers, outside of school, are my first-graders. But when they act like it. . . . Well, I've been called on it. "Remember, Steve, we're not in school any more," my wife says. "Don't treat me like your first-graders." (Interview, 3/11)

Steve's story suggests that we never quite get over ourselves as "the teachers." From Steve's, Gregg's, and my experiences, this submersion in the primary teaching culture can be a joyous experience. However, there were other perspectives among the men who taught in the primary grades.

RECONSIDERING CARE AS A MODEL FOR TEACHING

Teaching in the primary grades is essentially construed as a woman's domain, and men who work in this domain must negotiate their sameness or difference with this de facto reality. Of course, the negotiation of men in "a context of caring" is not unlike the negotiation and the personal adjustments that countless women have also had to make in relation to the culture of teaching. The decision to be a teacher and the decision to care may or may not be the same. It depends on the individual teacher. Men's enactment of both teaching and caring behaviors in primary classrooms may be seen by others as an atypical performance of gender-identified behavior. Therefore, it is useful to examine the reasons that primary education as caring has been considered to be women's work.

A critical approach to care behavior is followed by an examination of care's relationship to power. These perspectives are then used to examine teachers' relationships with children as people in child-centered classrooms. In concrete ways, the men who participated in this study spent considerable time and energy negotiating their own self-constructed "otherness." They saw themselves as different, and the need to be different from their colleagues was often manifested in ways that are similar to those Gilligan has discussed.

A Critical Perspective on Caring

As discussed in Chapter 2, much of the impetus for looking at caring as women's way of morality is based on the work of Gilligan (1982; Gilligan, Lyons, & Hanmer, 1990). *In a Different Voice* is Gilligan's (1982) response to Kohlberg's (1981) stages of moral development. In contrast to the Kohlberg model, justice and individualism are not the only determinants of social morality. Gilligan presents a "care perspective" as an alternative social morality that includes a social network of interconnected relationships. This network is sustained by communication. Gilligan maintains that a care perspective is based on affection, affiliation, contextual factors, and relationships. For the men who position themselves, or are positioned by others, outside this network of care and the talk that sustains it, the support for their teaching is compromised. In an ethic of care, resolutions of moral dilemmas are based on relationships as they are perceived throughout the crises. These resolutions include decisions based on socially connected conceptions of morality. Socially grounded resolutions contrast with a formal, decontextualized, or individualized logic of justice or fairness. Contextually based resolutions are less likely to be made by the "lone wolf" or "rugged individual" teacher, male or female, who closes the door and works with his or her kids. If teachers also decline to eat lunch with colleagues or restrict their affiliations in similar ways, then their connections are limited and their access to help and support are reduced.

While caring itself is not essentialized as feminine by Gilligan, she does suggest that morality based on an ethic of care is one that tends to be female. Participants in this study would agree with Gilligan (emphatically).

Caring is viewed by these teachers as "good teaching." Conversely, Gilligan suggests that a morality based on justice and individualism is more likely to be male. Interestingly, the men in this study also tended to view the disciplining of children as a matter of individual competence, although they often refused invitations to discipline others' students.

In terms of moral development, Gilligan (1987) suggests that children know both caring and justice orientations and can readily frame and solve moral problems in both of these ways. This means that the framing of moral problems is itself an element of moral decision making. Using a Vygotskian perspective, Gilligan argues that children are born into helplessness and inequality. They are less capable and less powerful. As such, they necessarily depend on the authority and the goodwill of their parents. Therefore, the consistent striving of children is for greater power, equality, and autonomy. Following Chodorow (1978), Gilligan argues that mothers encourage their girl children to identify with them in a "one-connected" relationship, whereas boy children experience a tension with their mother in an "other-unconnected" relationship. From this early conditioning emerges the sense of self as "one-caring" or the absence of "one-caring."

One can readily see the limits in the essentialist reasoning that prescribes one kind of nurturing for infant girls and another for boys. It is, of course, important to avoid such essentialism regarding male and female roles and to keep the argument at the level of possible framings, or ways of understanding. The men who teach in the primary grades often referred to their gender-based differences as well as to their unique abilities to transcend that difference when working with the children.

Another Moral Dilemma

There are more fundamental principles at work beneath the male primary teachers' reported resistance to the gender stereotyping that marked their care as atypical for men. In fact, for many feminists, Gilligan's explanation of women' moral lives seems essentialist and creates the possibility of marginalizing the values of caring by making it a "women's" morality. For Code (1991):

> The problem is to devise alternatives [to idealist objectivity, i.e., masculinities] that neither presuppose "essential" femaleness nor appeal to "feminine" values that are just as unrealistically pure and unequivocal as ideal objectivity and masculinity. (p. 54)

Code (1991) further argues that both Kohlberg's *and* Gilligan's theories of moral development offer gender-coded qualities for males (e.g., objectivity, individuality) and females (e.g., connectedness, closeness) that are based on statistically minute segments of nonrepresentative groups (e.g., white, middle to upper class). Despite the fact that the selected population segments have "disproportionately large social influence" (p. 55), Code suggests that any generalizing of their moral reasoning to the entire population is risky business.

Beyond the issue of the participants' representativeness, Code (1991) questions the wisdom of dichotomizing a new feminine ethic of caring and responsibility against a traditional ethic of rights and justice. This separation seemingly exacerbates the existing binaries that have been constructed between

> duty and inclinations, public and private, reason and emotions and lead easily into the belief that the former [ethics of caring] or female morality, expresses the lesser, parochial concerns of women; [while] the latter [ethics of justice] or male morality, addresses the more serious, global concern of men. (p. 106)

The admission of a dichotomy has the possibility of reifying women's special and simultaneously subordinate status.

In its application to primary education, Code's critique would argue against female teachers as natural or otherwise axiomatic care providers. Similarly, our assumptions that male teachers *should* discipline would beg for discussion that would interrogate underlying beliefs. Fred's reluctance or inability to discipline also has multiple meanings. Further, Code opens the possibility of escaping our use of gender to delimit permissible sets of behaviors for males and females in general and for teachers specifically. To take the argument a step further, reading Code as a critic of the gender binary system, one might speculate that it is male primary grade teachers who might systematically provide opportunities for children's experimentation with "gender-appropriate" behaviors as well as models for other teachers' understanding of their own teaching.

Caring and Power

At this point, Code's (1991) arguments for a cautious interpretation of Gilligan's feminine morality as a subordinate state connect with several other theorists. Puka (1990, 1993) reconfigures the argument. From a perspective of care as liberation, he suggests that caring is not so much "a course of moral development, primarily, but a set of coping strategies for dealing with sexist oppression" (1990, p. 59). Puka suggests that rather than following a developmental model and articulating a "care maturity," we would do better to analyze caring as a "slave morality" and subsequently build an ethic of morality around how women, as subordinated members of this culture (and other cultures) rationalize their own victimization. Similar arguments are offered by Benhabib (1987), Broughton (1983), and Nails (1983). Gilligan's moral model of caring is therefore critiqued for affirming the status quo, for reinforcing current gender-based divisions of labor, and for foreclosing the remote possibility of social transformations that might emerge from considering alternative epistemologies of ethics, caring, and morality.

With the benefit of several earlier views, Tronto (1993) offers a comprehensive critique of Gilligan as well as an alternative vision. Rather that acquiescing to women's special abilities to care, Tronto suggests that caring is a set of related practices that include caring about, taking care of, caring for, and receiving caring. For Tronto, caring, in its multiple practices and all its intentions, is relegated to a subordinate status. Devaluing caring is not related to the act itself, nor to any of its constituent acts (about, for, of). Rather, Tronto suggests that the ways in which we socially construct "caring" devalue it. Yet within that devalued state, "caring about" and "taking care of" are acts associated with the more powerful, while "caring for" and "receiving caring" are done by the relatively less powerful.

Teachers' care for and about children, seen as a commodity or material object, initiates an economy of relations that eventually traps the teachers who care. Our care as teachers requires objects to receive our care. Caring for children, in Tronto's (1993) view, necessitates a less powerful constituency. In more traditional conceptions of teaching, where teachers were authorities, where we knew what students needed to know and evaluated when they "got it," such differentials of agency were less noticeable. Though power distribution, as viewed from a perspective of care, was as present as it ever was or is, it could not be seen. However, from a socioconstructivist perspective, the displacement of child autonomy through teachers' "care" is a real, tangible issue. Our desires to care for young students may cause us to delimit their activity. This may be prudent, productive, and healthy. It may also be restrictive, codependent, and unacknowledged. If children's development into independent adults is a goal, these relationships that are forged in a context of power transactions must be questioned.

In contrast to Gilligan's opposition to patriarchal morality, Tronto (1993) approaches caring from a patriarchy-as-cause-for-care perspective. Working from the stance that dominant groups tend to define the moral turf, Tronto concludes that "morality [and attendant caring] is always contextualized and historicized, even when it claims to be universal" (p. 62). It is on the issue of proclaimed universality that the moral development theories of both Kohlberg and Gilligan are taken to task. When morality is conceived hierarchically, as in the case of Kohlberg, progression in the hierarchy by *an individual* is always in relation to an "other." Therefore, such theory cannot ethically accommodate all actors. Tronto writes "that care is somehow tied to subordinate status in society is not inherent in the nature of caring, but is a function of the structure of social values and moral boundaries that inform our current ways of life" (pp. 62–63). To make this point, Tronto examines how the moral boundaries inherent in research by Kohlberg (educated, white, male) are reinstantiated by Gilligan (female, adolescent, white).

While Gilligan's model does not claim to be a gendered voice, readings by others of her work are fairly consistent in seeing it as a feminine construction of voice. Accordingly, Gilligan's developmental model, based on power and relationship as commodities, functions as a female universal theory of morality. Yet Tronto (1993) notes that when research similar to Gilligan's is conducted with less privileged groups, gender differences, if evident at all, are certainly less pronounced. So the not so subtle question becomes: Is it gender or power? For me, questioning Gilligan's thesis, which constructs care as feminine or females as caring, comes close to sexist arguments based on static gender roles. The trade is for a naturalized characterization of women, with innate capacity for caring. Taken up as an epistemology, capacity for care enacts a second-wave feminist philosophy, which can be read in opposition to earlier, more radicalized feminisms. The potential of this cohesive philosophy is to contain the victims in a circular reality. When women identify with an ethic of care, they align themselves with a subordinate group. As subordinate, their "unique" belief systems are devalued, and more powerful constituencies (men) can continue to dismiss them as "less than" and benefit from women's unpaid, or underpaid, care work. According to Tronto (1993):

> [That] the ethic of care, is nothing but a response to subordination makes sense if the ethic is viewed from the standpoint of the powerful. It also makes sense if the relatively powerless [Gilligan's idealized respondent] conceive of what they do from the standpoint of the powerful. (p. 89; the example is mine.)

In this way, Gilligan's moral theory functions as a transactional ideology. Because it tacitly acknowledges the primacy of hierarchy and universality (powerlessness and relationships), Gilligan's moral development theory delegitimized any critiques from marginal perspectives. Therefore moral pluralism—that is, recognition of many moralities—is equated with a "lesser morality."

It is interesting to compare this essentialist, universalist versus plurality debate in moral development with Heilbrun's (1988) conclusions about women's biography and autobiography. Having reached the conclusion that there did not exist an identifiable form for women's lives, Heilbrun recommended that women turn toward the center, value their own talk, and create textual forms to fit that talk. She also suggested that such a turn is a political gesture based on taking power away from a rhetorical cartel:

> To denounce women for their shrillness and stridency is another way of deny-ing them the right to power. Unfortunately, power is something that women abjure once they perceive the great difference between the lives possible to men and women, and the violence necessary to men to maintain their position of authority. . . . But however unhappy the concept of power and control may make idealistic women, they delude themselves if they believe that the world and the condition of the oppressed can be changed without acknowledging it. (p. 16)

Yet Tronto (1993) concludes that feminist separatism, as practiced by Gilli-gan and recommended by Heilbrun, may be encouraging outsiders' separat-ist morality rather than arguing for a gain in power by wresting it from the center. For teachers of young children, adopting an ethic of care as a pedagogical philosophy is not without costs. Some of the men in this study did choose to separate themselves from their female colleagues as well as the school social context. While they report suffering from the isolation, their individuality must be seen differently from that of their female col-leagues. Equating teaching with caring may, according to Tronto, keep it in a less valued, even disdained, status as a profession. And further, turning inward to develop a pedagogy based on care may not benefit those who believe and teach in caring ways, at least not from an outside view of the caring context.

Enacting Care While Teaching

When one reasons that primary teachers operate in a context of caring, or that teaching is caring, it is important to articulate how the construction of caring itself is formulated. From a perspective based on Gilligan, women's caring is natural, female, and obligatory. While certain women may not be adequate caregivers, this would surely reflect on their competence as women or teachers when caring behaviors signify "female" or "teacher." Similarly, caring by males might be a risky behavior vis-à-vis their masculine self-image and perception by others.

If the construction of caring in a teaching context is based on Tronto's theory of there being a subordinated set of behaviors, both men and women can work within a gender-neutral space to redefine social definitions of caring. Theoretically, these are minuscule points. Enacting the theory is more difficult still.

Based on their stories, the men who teach in the primary grades are frequently unable to leave gender signification out of the caring equation. Sometimes it involves their personal devaluing of the female-marked behaviors. Gender-based devaluation means that gossiping is done by women, it is marked and coded negatively by the men. At other times, they celebrate their own abilities to perform "things that women do." Of course, recognizing and proclaiming self, one can argue that we celebrate our female aptitudes in characteristically male ways. In either case, as the legacy of patriarchy, men can approach Code's (1991) rhetorical challenge "what can (s)he know?" with some reserve capital.

To pay the cost of this patriarchal bargain(?) is to be "in charge," "to (always) know," "and to be continuously responsible." These are the economies that drove Gregg from his first stint as a teacher. Working from Tronto's (1993) perspective, men who teach in primary grades may have a schizophrenic relationship to their work. One role, which we enact with our students, is caring for. It includes wiping noses, soothing fighters, and comforting parents. Another role is caring about, which we enact in a professional stance toward "the children" with our colleagues. These two stances, and the moderate level of dissonance they induce, are common to all primary teachers, male *and* female. Caring for others as a teaching act, while construed as a female orientation, is performed in similar ways by men who teach primary grades and by their female colleagues. In contrast, caring about may occur outside a face-to-face interaction and may also depend on the formation of an object to care about. There are subtle but important differences between men's and women's caring about. First, men are often expected to "care about" with authority, force, and discipline. Children, as students, are converted to objects or a single object (a class of students) that requires disciplining. The men in this study reported that they resisted such positioning. Second, in their "caring about" other teachers they frequently distanced themselves from female colleagues and devalued their perspectives in gender-defined ways (women's talk, inefficiency, and lack of knowledge). In this stance, female colleagues are made into an object group and subjected to sexist critique.

It is interesting to me that while men and women appear to interact with children in similarly patterned "women's ways," the men were not comfortable interacting with, or able to interact with, their colleagues in similarly constructed ways. However, it is not the case that the men never got along with female teachers. Several of the men who participated in this study mentioned close, collaborative female colleagues. Further, my critique offers only one side of an interaction. Certainly the female colleagues of the men teaching in the primary grades have perspectives that would both support and contrast with those of the men in this study. Nevertheless,

within women's ways of knowing and teaching—in this case, primary education—there is the potential for important philosophical differences between
men's and women's intentions to care.

Difference, in a postmodern sense, can be equated with the richness
available in diversity. Locating difference is a constructive and deconstructive project that leads to self-knowing. Knowing the self in a normative,
modernist context such as elementary schools is often achieved through
constructing and situating the "other," or "the one I am not." Yet for the
male teachers in this study who were testing normatively inscribed gender
roles, the shift in certain deployments of care, especially touch, was not
resolved through construction or through deconstruction.

TEACHING IS TOUCHING CHILDREN

Like many other beliefs, "We need more men in primary education" is one
that has its own set of problems. As unusual or marginal participants in a
women's context, men in primary contexts are monitored. As males who
also participate in a larger patriarchal culture, we have privileges that are
often less available to the women with whom we work. But privilege becomes baggage. One burden that follows us around is our sexuality. One
aspect of patriarchal culture is men's possession of autonomous sexuality. In
contrast, women's socially constructed sexuality has been absent, repressed,
and controlled (Fine, 1993). Such a privilege is baggage that becomes more
noticeable with a change of scene. While teaching, particularly with young
children, may be seen as virginal work (Waller, 1932), men are viewed as
sexualized in predatory ways in our culture. It is difficult to be a participant
in this "sacred trust" of caring for desexualized children (Kincaid, 1992)
when one is seen as sexually suspect. General presuppositions about males'
sexual agenda come into the classroom with men who teach in the primary
grades. And our personal constructions of "sexuality," of "teacher," and of
"child" cohabit a location called "touch." Teachers' touch, in particular male
teachers' touch, is the topic of much talk but the subject of little text (other
than newspaper scandals). The men who participated in this study talked
about the necessity of touch as part of teaching. They also talked about the
impossibility of touching children as part of teaching. The issues embedded
in this paradox are examined next.

Fear of Touching

Steve, as a young first-grade teacher, understood hugs as a ritualized
way of letting children know that he cared about them. As mentioned previously, this was a learned behavior for him, one he acquired by watching

women and by observing female teachers of young children. Yet he was simultaneously "scared that the kids will go home and say 'Mr. Norris touched me,'" especially when there are so many news stories about people being sued. It is ironic that after struggling with himself to be free to offer this affirmation to others, his hugging was now a "problem" in his teaching. He remembered his attempts to deal with his learning:

> [I was] uncomfortable in day care. All I did was walk around. Walk around. I couldn't sit down. I was afraid that they would sit on my lap. When I did flop down on the floor, I had about 30 kids sitting on me. After a while, I got used to it. (Interview, 4/13)

What Steve didn't realize at the time was that others had already decided what his sitting with and under children might mean. While Steve may have gotten used to children sitting on him, other adults have not gotten used to it. Steve has an understanding about his physical contact with children. In one way or another, the male primary teachers acknowledged that there was a great deal of hysteria and fear about teachers' touching children and the talk about it.

Van related to this issue very directly. As a first-year teacher of first-graders at age 45, he accepted the conditions. He suggested:

> Some behavior women exhibit, such as hugging, is acceptable for just women. I have to watch how I behave toward students. Girls come up and hug me. I let them, and then push them away. I can't really hug them back . . . I don't want it to go any further than just a simple hug. I constantly monitor [myself]. . . . It goes with the job. (Interview, 3/7)

Van believed that he should not have any physical contact with children. While he realized that children have emotional and physical needs that are met through physical contact, he was unable to provide for that need. "Going further" in his descriptions suggests that such a place indeed exists and points to the pervasive presence of the idea of molestation in our teaching culture. He is resigned to living with the tension created by this paradox of care. He continued:

> I think that there will always be a fear that any man on the staff is there only for one reason, and that's to get at some kid. It's because it's in the news. I think it's blown way out of proportion. It's not going to change. It's part of the job. (Interview, 3/7)

Van identified an underlying cultural bias that men who work with children are interested in sexual contact with them. He further extrapolated the

reasoning that potential sexual abusers in the teaching profession are defined exclusively by their presumed sexual desire. That is, men who are
thought to be interested in sex with children can't simultaneously be thought
of as otherwise effective, or as simply "people with a problem," or as capable
teachers. From my experiences as a teacher and a teacher educator, Van's
characterizations of others' perceptions about sexually abusive teachers
seem reflective of reality, but his consistent refrain, "It's part of the job," also
shows a tolerance of others' sexual innuendo.

What Van did understand was that what is permissible teaching is
highly circumscribed around these ritualized enactments of our tacitly
shared perspectives of adult male sexuality (pervasive) and childhood sexuality (absent). He knows that public display or, even worse, observed covert
display of "inappropriate" behavior is behavior that can cost a job and a
reputation. But "inappropriate" is another one of those subjective places we
tacitly refuse to examine.

> I cannot show the same affection as a woman can because it's inappro-
> priate behavior for a man. I know that. So, I don't do that. It's what
> other people think. I can lose my job. And all that would take is "He
> looked at me funny." (Interview, 4/13)

Van's fear was about misrepresentation of his behaviors costing him his
job. In this locale, during this time, several teachers have lost their teaching
positions because of various transgressions involving sexual, verbal, or drug
abuse. Although none of the teachers were in elementary grades, the threat
of job loss, the fear of accusations about his behavior as a teacher, are
everyday experiences for Van.

The fears and coping strategies of Van and the other study participants
were consistent with other teachers' understanding of the normative pressures on their teaching behavior (King, Danforth, Perez, & Stahl, 1994). In
working with female elementary teachers, King and colleagues (1994) found
that there existed for each elementary teacher a set of "appropriate" behaviors and, more important, a set of "inappropriate" behaviors. Engaging in
inappropriate behavior while teaching can get you "the ax." Teachers defined the ax as any limiting of their teaching behavior, including job loss.
The ax could come from parents or principals, but apparently not from
principles. Social construction of the ax is based on taking risks with "inappropriate behavior." But rather than acting on risky principles, teachers
worked within a self-imposed set of delimited behaviors, thereby avoiding
the "external ax" but acquiring a permanently affixed "internal ax." Van's

realizations create for him a safety zone, guarded by such an ax. He considered the consequences:

> I have to be rather insensitive to these kids. I don't like to be, but I could lose my job. Say, I was spending extra time with a little girl who just lost her father, whether through divorce or death, I could actually help her through a tough time by being a father figure. But others [adults] might say "Why is he spending so much time with that little girl?" It puts me at a disadvantage. (Interview, 4/13)

As an experienced teacher, Gregg's reaction to the implicit intimidation was much different from Van's. While he acknowledged the same conditions, he reasoned: "For a while, [touch] was a real big issue. At the beginning of the year they try to scare you. Talk and stories about lawsuits. It doesn't affect me that much" (Interview, 4/11). Gregg located the source of the "touch hysteria" (Johnson, 1995, 1997) in the school and suggested that this political use of touch was a purposeful insertion into the school culture. Perhaps in so understanding, and with some experience, he was able to pay less attention to it. Another experienced teacher, Ken, also realized the situation involved multiple issues, and he continued to teach in ways he saw as "appropriate for children" but perhaps risky for himself. "I've never been accused of anything in 17 years of [kindergarten] teaching."

Steve's understanding of the prohibition against hugging men gets to some of the underlying issues of gender and sexuality: "Society allows men to hug children at home. But outside of home, men don't hug children or other men. They hug women" (Interview, 4/13). If men's public hugging is for women, Steve's parameters for hugging included an implicit argument that hugging was sexually informed touching. Of course, the implication essentializes all intimacy between genders as sexual and, by extension, all physical contact as an overture to sexual activity. We all recognize the stretch these overgeneralizations place on the reasoning and intellectually reject them. Yet the fallout from this deeply rooted, irrational reasoning is that men think hugging is for sex, and that all of us, men and women, think that men think that hugging is sex. If that chain of reasoning is true, then men hugging children *is* inappropriate. Yet few, if any, would object to men touching their own children. Why is it, then, that women are permitted physical contact with others' children and men are not? Whatever the men who teach in the primary grades say that they feel about touch and the hysteria that centers around it, they all have systematic ways, or rules, that condition their use of touch when they teach.

Rules of Touch and Places for Intimacy

Steve's rules consisted of how his touch was given and where and when it was appropriate. Characterizing the nature of touching, he said: "My hugs are side hugs. I stand next to them. I also pat them on the head, pat them on the back" (Interview, 4/13). Steve's hugs and pats were in safe zones. Patting kids' heads was not the same as touching their faces. Side hugs circumvented the possibility of any genital contact. He also used hug substitutes such as positive feedback. "Nice job. I like the way you are thinking." After learning to hug, Steve had to rethink and reschedule how his learned behavior was to be used.

> I let them [the students] know I was very open. I said "If you want to give Mr. Norris a hug, it's OK. Mr. Norris will hug you back. If you don't want to, Mr. Norris understands." You know, I just let them know it was OK either way. (Interview, 3/11)

Gregg's rules define situations and social spaces where touch and hugging are acceptable in his teaching. He explains:

> I have two or three little girls who come to class early and, of course, I can't let them in the room alone with me. They must wait outside the room. When I *am* in the room with a few students, I always leave the door open. I'm just watching my back. (Interview, 4/11)

By saying "of course," Gregg indicated that these understandings were, in his view, common knowledge. Indeed, I am aware of them. I am also aware that some women teach within these same behavioral rules. Gregg's use of strategic behavior, such as leaving the classroom door open to "cover his back," reveals the extent to which others' perceptions of our touch invades our teaching spaces and psyches. What Gregg's back gets covered with is the gaze of potential observers. Under a self-imposed threat of surveillance, Gregg and the other participants withheld hugging. Hugs, as commodities, were available only at certain times of the day, co-occurring with specified rituals.

Steve explained his rules:

> I don't hug them when they come in early [early arriving students]. They sharpen pencils, get a book, use the restroom . . . hugs happen when leaving, arriving [in groups]. I hug them as a group during the day. Less often, I hug them before special subjects, when they leave for

or return from lunch, or on the way to the bus. In the morning, I greet them by name. (Interview, 5/7)

Like his use of women's ways of teaching, Steve's use of hugging was situationally specified and functionally grounded. Students were ritually hugged as part of a group of students, especially when they arrived in or departed from the classroom. Unspoken, but highly evident in contrast, was the rule that individual students were never hugged in isolation. He understands how and when hugging is acceptable. Steve also understands that some primary teachers, male and female, are not huggers. Further, even talking about hugs was not normal male behavior outside the school. For me, the specificity of Steve's rules was a sign that they were important. Yet Steve's rules, while more clearly articulated than those given by most of the other male primary teachers, were a prototype.

In explaining his development of rules for touch, Gregg referred to gender. He thought that formation of gender and differences in its public performance heavily influenced his rules of touching:

It's easier for women to be open. For a man to be sensitive and open with children, people see it as strange. "Why is he doing this? Why is he always touching my child?" Whereas when women do it, it's OK. I'm not angry. I just feel left out and discriminated against because I can't be as open with a child as a woman is. (Interview, 6/5)

Gregg's comments raise several issues. "Why is he always doing this?" uses one word—"always"—to imply the intended impropriety. The discourse of slander and accusation is subtle. It raises a question of differences in intimacy between home and school. It also raises the question of differences in gestures of intimacy between genders. While as teachers we talk about developing caring relationships with children, there are limits to our physical expression of that care. Ours expressions of care are much more carefully made than those of parents. Furthermore, while media portrayals of men's interaction with children are changing toward more instances of men's sensitive interaction, that same intimacy is not available to men who teach young children. But I do not mean to suggest that these men and myself should do our work any differently in the current circumstances. What I am suggesting is that it is critical to realize what a large part this thinking plays in our daily decisions about children and teaching them. As a group, the men talked about checking on open doors, arranging conferences so that other adults could see in, and close monitoring of appropriate touch.

Teachers and Accusations of Improper Touch

Men who teach young children within Noddings's (1992) and Nias's (1989) ideologies of "teaching as care" may be at risk. Anderson's (1919/1966) powerful narrative "Hands" details the costs of a man who cares for children in teaching contexts. In writing about Wing's years as a teacher, Anderson describes him as "meant by nature to be a teacher of youth. He was one of those rare, little men who rule by a power so gentle that it passes as a lovable weakness" (p. 31).

Anderson creates in his character, Wing, the power to teach, care, and change lives through touch.

> Here and there went his hands, caressing the shoulders of the boys, playing about the tousled heads. As he talked his voice became soft and musical. There was a caress in that also. In the way the voice and hands, the soft stroking of the shoulders and the touching of the hair were parts of the schoolmaster's efforts to carry a dream into the young minds. By the caress that was in his fingers he expressed himself. He was one of those men in whom the force that creates life is diffused, not centralized. Under the caress of his hands, doubt went out of the minds of the boys and they began also to dream. (pp. 32–33)

But Wing's touch of the students is understood differently by the townspeople. Through the character of the saloon keeper, who beats and kicks him, Wing is warned, "I'll *teach you* to put your hands on my boy, you beast" (p. 32; emphasis added) and "Keep your hands to yourself" (p. 33). Wing is driven from the town and endures his shamed hands by keeping them out of sight and himself away from others. He becomes a recluse. I'm intrigued by the choice of Anderson's words "I'll teach you" spoken by the attacker. The "teaching" enacted by the saloon keeper is brutal, abusive, and criminal. It was not so long ago that corporal punishment was a common teaching tool. Physical abuse of children in school contexts (e.g., paddling) has historically been tolerated to a greater degree than has caring touch.

In "Hands" Anderson uses the character of Wing to teach readers about the injustices of misinterpreting touch and misunderstanding others' caring. Wing is victimized by a misrepresentation that was born of bigotry and fear. Yet when I was rereading the previously quoted paragraph, I recoiled at the words *caress* and *stroking*. These intimate physical acts of caring made me uncomfortable when I read them and now when I write them. I thought about how I use my hands as a teacher. I have told myself that touch is a productive and ethical teaching move. I have conditioned my hands that they only touch my students on their shoulders, arms, and upper backs. I have further instructed my hands that touch means quick pats, not massage.

Like the participants in the study and the rules of touch they constructed, I think my rules of touching in classrooms are productive ones. I do not mean to suggest that I, or other teachers, should touch in ways that are different from my rules. But it is important to question why touching is so suspect a behavior that it requires rules to constrain it. Controlling teachers' touch through a tacit set of social understandings is complex. Embedded in this complexity is the unspoken but palpable accusation of pedophilia. Making accommodation to this accusation is part of the identity formation for men who choose to teach in the primary grades. The issues surrounding the political use of sexual identities is explored in Chapter 12.

TEACHING IS CARE: A SUMMARY

Teaching in the primary grades has been equated with care. While essentializing complex teaching decisions, the equation teaching = care provides a lens into that complexity. If care is a domain of relationships that is ascribed to women, then men's enactment of care behavior will be marginalized and, as shown in this study, viewed with suspicion. Specifically, men's use of touch as care was seen by all of us, especially these participants, as risky behavior. Yet touch is such an integral part of a teaching repertoire that these participants, as well as other teachers, male and female, continue to use physical touch as part of teaching. This use, however, is constrained by a rationalized set of rules for the deployment of touch.

The use of care as a model for teaching is not without philosophical, ethical, and economic objections. Women's use of care, as a naturally occurring attribute, has been used against women's claims for professional status as teachers. Men's choice to participate in relatively less valued work can be seen as a threat to a patriarchal set of work transactions.

The behaviors that are seen as care as well as the intention to perform them are associated with women. Men's performance of these behaviors involves crossing the gender borders. The next chapter examines men's teaching from a gender perspective.

CHAPTER 11

Gender Work: Men Teaching in Women's Ways

One way of looking at men's work in the primary grades is from a perspective of cross-gendered behavior. The participants in this study were men who were working in a women's professional field. And while this investigation of those men's awareness of and accommodation to their atypical work is revealing, using gender as a point of view is not without problems.

PROBLEMS WITH A GENDER LENS

First, understanding men's experiences within "gender-appropriate" and "gender-inappropriate" categories continues what I believe to be a mistaken dichotomy between gender and constructions of what constitutes "appropriate behavior" for teachers. In fact, a paradox of this analysis is that these men were conducting "test cases" of men's work in women's work space. So to look at their work from a gendered perspective seems counter to their goal. It seems more reasonable to try to understand primary teachers' behavior, male and female, from a feminist perspective because primary teaching is a female context. A feminist perspective is also reasonable because critical deconstruction of gendered social practice is not only possible but also necessary within feminism.

A second rationale for the use of gender is the participants' investment in the topic. During interviews, the men repeatedly spoke about the lack of correspondence between the biological sex of teachers and desirable behaviors for primary teachers in their relationships with children. I understood this talk as the participants' reframing the identity politics from "good girl" to "good teacher." In such a shift, the issue of *should* men be doing this work is reframed. Instead the question becomes, Should people with or without certain qualities or competencies be teaching young children?

Reversing the argument again, the considerable attention that was given gender by the men could be seen as a way of avoiding other underlying issues, such as competence, experience, pay, and energy, to mention a few of the points of potential difference between male and female teachers. As examples of the resistant deployment of gender factors, this chapter presents the men's talk about other teachers (who were female), which was characteristically framed in gendered dichotomies. Usually, the gender dichotomies—such as men are efficient in meetings; women are not—were broached by the men in essentialist ways that blamed social differences on the biological sex of the teachers. Thus, in the above example, inefficiency is a "natural" aspect of being female.

Finally, to use gender itself as a "reality" rather than a provisional construction is problematic because once "it" exists (and it does), then expectations for male and female behaviors inform and bias interpretations of behavior. And in these male spaces of interpretation that were used by the male primary teachers in this study, the demons of femininophobia broke in, shaped thinking, and informed valuing, particularly regarding teaching that was done by females.

There was a dichotomy in the way the male primary teachers in my study looked at their work as women's work. On one hand, they denied that the work itself was female and claimed that the fact that they did their work well was proof that men could do it. Therefore, teaching young children shouldn't be just for women. On the other hand, they systematically devalued what they perceived as "women's stuff" that occurred within this context. It is ironic that the men allowed themselves the opportunity to perform caring teaching acts without the stigma of feminine devaluing. But these same behaviors were critiqued by the men in the study when they were done by female teachers. Perhaps it is not even ironic. Perhaps it is again "business as usual."

It becomes difficult for me to know whether the belief systems evidenced in the men's comments are new social attitudes toward masculinity, postfeminist sexism, or my delusions. In a previous semester, I taught a seminar in feminist critical literacy to a group of 10 female doctoral students. For the first two weeks of the semester, they declined my invitations to comment, to react, or to critique the readings by Valerie Walkerdine, Pam Gilbert, and Elizabeth Long that I had chosen for the course. In the third week I learned that they had little use for (my) feminism: "Feminism has already happened. We've done this." My response was to privately belittle the students because they were not feminists. I resorted to sexist "putdowns" to cover my hurt and embarrassment (King, 1992).

In many ways, the male primary teachers' appropriation of feminine teaching practices was like my trying to teach feminist literary theory: We were all making objects of the female teachers in order to understand our difference from "them." I had implicitly asked my female doctoral students to become objects of the course scrutiny. Similarly, the men in this study objectified their female colleagues in order to understand their own roles as teachers. To me, both are examples of provisional or false consciousness.

COMPARISONS WITH WOMEN'S TEACHING

Gregg became aware that his teaching of young children was not satisfying him. He reasoned that the problem was his lack of affective involvement with his students, which he saw as a personal problem and a problem for his students. He began a personal transformation toward more nurturing relationships with his second-graders:

> I was worried what people around me thought. The perception is that men don't play that female role. It's OK if a father hugs, but society doesn't think men should be affectionate with [other people's] children. (Interview, 4/11)

All of the participating male primary teachers at least acknowledged awareness that their career choice was seen as one that "women do." Further, most discussed the attributes and behaviors of primary teachers, and specifically their teaching roles, as characteristically feminine. In each case in which we thought about those attributes of their teaching, as two men, it was important enough for us to talk through, several times for each informant, how each of us understood that this work was not "just for women." Paul's decision (Chapter 4) to leave lucrative employment to become a teacher-in-training, one who eats peanut butter sandwiches, is emblematic of the degree to which the men had planned for this work as rightfully theirs.

Gregg recognized that others might categorize many of his teaching acts as "female." He spoke softly to his students, he held their hands, and he hugged them. In discussing how he understood the risks he was taking, he acknowledged others' possible misinterpretations, but he didn't feel at risk. "These aren't female behaviors. They are good teaching. I hope that we have evolved enough to realize that we can be whoever we are and not worry about what 'gender' our behavior is" (Interview, 4/11). He also had a sense of conviction about his role as a primary teacher. He was able to fall back on that reserve of confidence when he talked about his teaching as "risky behavior":

> Look, I know what I'm doing. After several years in primary, I know that children respond to certain behavioral styles more appropriately

than to other behavioral styles. If that kind of teaching is seen as female by someone else, that's not my problem. (Interview, 4/11)

Gregg's reasoning is at once defiant and centered on children. For me, this
is characteristic of many decisions made by teachers in general and by these
male primary teachers specifically. Resistance is "for the sake of the kids."
And it can be contrasted with descriptions of primary teachers' lack of
voicing of their own needs (Nias, 1989).

Often, working in a women's world, the men who taught in the primary
grades chose to isolate themselves socially. Rather than socialize with
women, they don't socialize; but this is not a consistent resolution. Ken
remembered that some years ago he had to choose a social group for himself
during faculty meetings. The men in the school sat at one table. "[I] had to
choose whether or not to sit with the men at faculty meetings. I decided to
sit with smokers [instead] and my best friend. But I still wondered if I
shouldn't be sitting 'with the guys'" (Interview, 4/5). Comparing a chain of
connected memories, Ken then returned to his childhood, and a Thanksgiv-
ing dinner with his family, when he was faced with a similar choice: watching the football game with the men or talking with the women in the
kitchen. Likewise, monitoring teaching behaviors because someone else
might see them as female is a constant issue. Yet the behaviors that signify
a "caring teacher" may also be read as female. If gender is flexible, as
several of the men in this study claimed, then there shouldn't be a status
difference for male *or* female attributes. Butler (1990), Plummer (1991), and
Weeks (1985) argue that gender (maleness, femaleness) is a social construction. It is so regularized that we begin to see gender as "natural" and tied to
a specific or appropriate biological sex. Yet all three of the theorists remind
us that such compulsory attribution is a clear indicator of the energy bound
up in maintaining these gender dichotomies. Their shared point is that this
constructed difference is a mechanism for the perpetuation of "natural difference," which allows for dominance.

These examples from interviews also point out that the participants'
reaction to seeing themselves in others' stories as female is varied. In the
context of an elementary school, the male primary teachers reported
greater comfort with their teaching performances. But similar behaviors—
such as touch, gossip, and caring, were seen as problematic in contexts
outside of school. It is safe to say that what is seen as "feminine" is, in part,
a function of the context. Or, if the context is decidedly feminine, then
behavioral expectations for men may be more female but still not the same
as for females. However, the neat dichotomy implied in situationally fixed
values for particular behaviors is not so neat. For example, Van was a
foreman in a boilerworks before he came to teaching. He characterized

himself as a "caring foreman" and saw himself as somewhat distinctive in this regard when compared with workmates in similar positions. Further troubling the dichotomy of caring only inside teaching contexts was the previously mentioned pattern of the male primary teachers' employment in other caring professions, such as elder care, preschool child care, and hospital care.

Ken's explanation for gendered teaching feels like a touchstone for my own experiences. According to Ken:

> The men who do a real good job in primary [teaching] identify with women and perhaps spent their time as kids hanging out with women. They relate to women, and they relate to women's tasks. Whereas the men who are the lone wolves are trapped between two worlds. They are uncomfortable in a social system that is nurturing, but their economic situation is dependent upon them being there. (Interview, 4/5)

Even more explicitly, Ken sums up with: "You'll find that what is a good teacher in early childhood is tied into a female stereotype." Recognizing these conditions and working through them, on a daily basis, was the subject of much of the male primary teachers' talk about gendered teaching behavior. The participants reacted differently to balancing what it means to be male while doing female work in a female work space.

RESISTANCE TO WOMEN'S WAYS

The male primary teachers made accommodations to women's ways of knowing and teaching in primary grade classrooms and in the larger school context. Yet there were many patterns of resistance to what were identified as "women's ways" of doing school.

Competing with Women

Steve viewed the whole thing as a challenge. "I can do it (better)" seemed to be his motto. The "better" often set him apart, and he was resented at times. Steve's "doing it better" may not match his female colleagues' ways of doing things. Other teachers' resentment toward Steve can be understood as his not fitting what Gilligan (1982) described as women's connected knowing and their resistance to morally risky acts of self-promotion. Steve explicitly reveals himself as in competition to be the best. With such individualism, Steve claimed an authority about knowing that is also in contrast to the taxonomy proposed by Belenky et al. (1986) of ways that women more typically know. So, both morally and epistemologically, Steve is different. For the most part, Steve looked at teaching like a series of merit badges and proudly wore each accomplishment.

> When I make a shirt [stenciled T-shirt], or make brownies and bring them in, I'll get comments like "Oh, did your wife make that?" And I always say "No, if my wife wasn't even there, I still would have made it myself." (Interview, 4/13)

When Steve dramatized the role of the doubting female teacher, he raised the pitch of his voice, which I interpreted as a whine. He not only pointed out the inaccuracy of his colleagues' assumptions; he also intended to undermine them with his parody. Steve acknowledged the communication problems that he has in conversations with colleagues in which they test gender-appropriate behaviors.

> The first time I said this this year, I think I offended the lady. Everyone assumes my wife made it [T-shirt with stenciled design]. She doesn't know anything about the Ellison machine [which cuts stenciled shapes]. I made it myself. I made the cake. I made the brownies. I made the shirt. I made the cookies. I *can* bake! And I don't want them to assume that because I'm married that my wife does all my baking, all my sewing, and all my T-shirts, and stuff. (Interview, 4/13)

Steve was proud of his accomplishments. Consequently, he was hurt and angry when he was not given credit for these projects. Steve's value for an image as an independent and competent teacher surpassed his fears about others' devaluing his skills because they are usually tasks undertaken by women. For him, it was important to be seen as a competent teacher. He wanted credit for his acquired skills, even if this risked possible discredit by other teachers with more traditional values of gendered behavior.

Steve was also interested in what he and other male teachers wore in the classrooms and in the rules that create and limit their clothing options. As he wrote in Chapter 5, he planned to develop a specialized line of clothing for male teachers in the primary grades. Steve's desire to wear shorts or sleeveless shirts seemed less an agenda for fashion and comfort than a test case in gender-specified permissible behaviors for men in the primary grades. In this way, his fashion interest is like his culinary interest.

It is interesting to look at Steve's responses to others' questions about his trials with behaviors attributed to females in his teaching repertoire. He made some decisions about which female-identified behaviors were justifiable and which were not. Jewelry was not OK, but shorts and possibly sleeveless shirts were. Baking food for children and their parents was fine, but eating food with other women was not. For me, his decisions about appropriateness center on their functional relationship with his students. Regardless of the gender inscription on the particular behavior, whether it was used or not used depended on how it would affect on his work with kids. In this way, shorts were justified as more comfortable for his active teaching. Shouting angrily was not justifiable, and artistic expression must have a logical, functional rationale. Not all valuing decisions that are made, however, are based on so logical an array of decisions.

Textual Dependance and Active Learning

Cal saw his kindergarten curriculum as one centered on movement and activity as well as derived from direct experiences. These aspects made it a "physical, masculine curriculum." He recalled "set-ups," wherein the arranged physical environments that he designed induced certain desired learning goals. When Cal planned for his students' practice with polite forms of speech, he organized an activity center that necessitated students sharing. He resisted the mediated curriculum of text, which he related to women's functional dependence on authority. "Reliance on textbooks is a female dependance thing."

Cal combined the constructs of care, text, and dependence into a curricular sweep. In first grade, the freedom that kids enjoyed as kindergartners ends. Desks are assigned and "the book comes out." In one of our interviews he explained, "In one summer [between kindergarten and first grade] kids automatically mature to sitting in a seat all day" (Interview, 5/10). Cal is concerned that rather than a context of caring, primary education can also be seen as a "matriarchal machine." The vast majority of elementary teachers are female. As a result, according to Cal, "We are hearing an overwhelmingly feminine voice in opinions and decision making." At this point, I responded to Cal defensively and wondered to myself why we bother to label our teaching male or female. Then he reeled me back in with an interesting argument. In curriculum, Cal reasoned, women favor a language arts–based approach. As we talked, Cal's theory of "female curriculum" unfolded. He later wrote out his thoughts on curriculum and its relationship to gender (see Chapter 8).

According to Cal, women prefer to use a mediated reality based on a textual representation of experience rather than the experience itself. When experiences do occur or are even arranged, they are created for the purposes of generating texts, which will then be used as a mediating context that will contain the lesson. I am reminded of the Language Experience Approach (Stauffer, 1980) to reading and writing instruction and the whole-language movement (Goodman, 1986) in literacy. In using these approaches and advocating that others use them, I understood my intentions as centering on children's literacy development for the purposes of their empowerment. What Cal suggested to me was that such a move may not be so altruistic and certainly not without consequences. I now recognize the possibility of appropriating children's lives as occasions to train them in literacy.

Cal maintained that teachers' adherence to a textual curriculum bows to authority and doesn't involve the risk of independence and creativity. Because text is a mediated reality, it can be contained and controlled. Now I am reminded of Silin's (1995) argument that in resisting a technical vocabulary, elementary teachers resist external regulation. But what of these same teachers who infuse their students with a technical control over language? At the point of teachers' construction of error and accuracy in children's writing and reading (King & Barksdale-Ladd, 1995), are they not controlling reality, just as they are controlled? Children's behavior is more managed, more predictable for the teachers' control. Teachers' behavior is now more managed and more predictable (Shannon, 1989). I understand this as Cal's definition of prescribed or sanctioned ways of teaching. Because of (mostly female) teachers' preference for the text, language arts and reading consume large amounts of the available class time. According to Cal, the reason boys more often than girls are seen as in need of remediation is because they are experiencing a "curriculum hung on the word" and its delivery, as mediated by women.

Cal's arguments are similar to those proposed in the early 1970s. As an early reaction to feminism, writers in education began to question the possible deleterious effects of exclusively female teachers in the elementary grades. At the time, the discussion was framed as a comparison of what men and women offered young children as their teachers. Unlike the expanded notions of "feminine" lives that feminism attempted to offer to women, men were not part of the "expansion" of possible lives. The analysis did not engage the notion that men and their masculinities might also be a flexible relationship.

"Education is the power in you to teach. But people [and texts] telling you what to do is disempowering. It's more like others telling you what to do." Cal explicitly understood these teaching differences between his approach and those of female colleagues in terms of gender. He was confident that boys are less successful because they don't have sufficient (any) male guidance in schools:

> Girls do better in early years because they have female teachers. This
> is disastrous for boys. They want hands-on [activities]. They are not in-

terested in abstract words. . . . Boys are hurting for more than just a language approach and need more hands on learning. (Interview, 5/10)

It seems problematic to me that only boys would want concrete experience and that only girls would enjoy language. And, of course, the same questions of gender match apply to teachers as well. The argument was repeatedly reflected in the 1970s gender studies of teachers. In general, the call for men to enter elementary teaching was based on the belief that young boys were being shortchanged or damaged by exclusively female teachers. In Robinson's (1981, 1986) reviews of men as primary grade teachers, he cites a debate during the 1970s that centered on simplistic, essentialist notions of males and females with fixed gender identities. Sciarra (1974) and Smith (1973), as well as many others, argued that the presence of men would ameliorate the feminization of young male students. For the most part, these concerns were quelled with claims of gender relativism and appeals to sound teaching practice that was not essentially male or female. Yet, based on Cal's understanding of the meaning of his work with children, there are at least isolated teachers who maintain that teachers' and students' genders do affect learning in deleterious and patterned ways.

Another issue embedded in the suggestion that young boys need men as teachers is the fact that young girls also need them for the same reasons. Further, to suggest that women, some women, all women cannot provide "male-type" activities for children is also an untested assumption. And finally, when we hold that some activities in the classroom are "male" and some are "female," we forfeit our chances to reduce the influence of prescriptive gender roles in children's social development.

Curriculum and the Psychological

In terms of interactions with students, Cal saw being female as a problem. "Women . . . try to appease children. Men want to deal in reality, not deal with the psychological. I'm not a teacher of individual problems" (Interview, 6/5). Cal restated his point that women teachers are overly involved in the "psychological lives" of their students:

> Females are too attached to kids. They want to know their kids inside and out. I don't see it that way. I want to teach the curriculum. It's a whole different way of thinking. . . . It's a motherly instinct of wanting close attention and attachments with kids. (Interview, 6/5)

I find myself agreeing with Cal's last point, but with a different set of reasons for valuing for it. I agree, it's a whole different approach. Perhaps part of the difference can be found in the word *curriculum*. For Cal, and for other teachers I know, curriculum is the knowledge base, the academic, intellectual commodity that is to be delivered, planted, and grown. In a passive learning mode, Cal's model for teaching is like Freire's (1968) banking metaphor, used to signify passive learners who are seen as storage containers for knowledge. In such a teacher- and knowledge-centered approach to learning, the curriculum occupies an important position. The learners are expected to deliver that same static knowledge on demand.

In fact, all teachers must attend to the intellectual material in their teaching. If prescribed content, as curriculum, is encountered more actively by students, teachers may appear to subscribe to child-centered learning. Yet there remains the prescription of knowledge itself. How much of a leap must we make to arrive at canonical dictionaries of culture? For me, the decisions we make between content and students seem a matter of centering. For the majority of primary teachers, whether male or female, curriculum centers on the developing child. For the stakeholders in a child-centered perspective, it is possible to understand knowing students inside and out. In fact, the degree to which I can accomplish this may be seen as a benchmark for my proficiency as a primary grade teacher. Yet it doesn't seem necessary or productive to differentiate a curriculum for each gender. Consider the following thoughts, a restatement from an interview with Cal: "Curriculum is a very different thing epistemologically for women than it is for men. Women focus on relationships and center on children. Men focus on curriculum and the class as a group" (Interview, 6/5).

But curriculum isn't "this" or "that." Pinar (1975) has suggested that the construct *currere* may be more reflective of experiences with the integrated and interactive nature of what we are referring to as curriculum, rather than the object curriculum itself. Teachers help their students "to travel [to study] with wise companionship." But "before we learn to teach in such a way, we must learn how to learn in such a way . . . we teachers . . . must become students of currere, which is to say students of ourselves" (p. 412).

We know that differences in perspective toward curriculum exist within education generally and within primary education in particular. In fact, differences in focus occurred within the group of male primary teachers. Certain perspectives have historically been allocated to one or other gender. But whether individual men or women hold a female-identified, child-centered view of their own teaching is not so easy to determine. Further, teachers' espoused and self-perceived curricular orientations may not be the ones that they act on in context. Having danced around this issue and Cal's clear arguments, it is also important to acknowledge that his approach to curriculum is shared by many other teachers, although, in my experience, few in the primary grades and a minority in this study.

Teaching Responsibility

Cal argued that men as teachers are more prepared to assume responsibility for their own class of students:

Young children need structure and discipline, not coddling . . . one person taking responsibility, rather than sending kids all over [for a] "plugin" education! I feel like I'm in charge of the class. (Interview, 6/5)

Cal's analysis related class size and overcrowding to women's unwillingness to be responsible for their students. In a lengthy discussion of site-based management and a goal of lower teacher–pupil ratios, he reasoned that support personnel represent female teachers unwillingness to own their responsibility for their students. Cal suggested that if so much money were not tied up in support personnel, a teacher might have as few as 15 children in a class and then be able to provide for their needs independently.

While Cal did acknowledge the needs of the students and the teacher's role in meeting those needs, he refused to acknowledge that his perspective is one that turns on a dynamo of gender and sexism. Because there are so few men in primary grade teaching, he maintained that it is irrelevant for a man to talk about "women" and his difference from them. "In a whole sea of women's faces, we [male teachers] don't bother to see ourselves as 'not female.'" Rather, his differences from his female colleagues may be realized as not having a certain characteristic, such as nurturing. The characteristic is an acknowledged aspect of successful teaching, but it may be compromised by Cal's masculinity. Likewise, a female colleague may happen to be less accomplished at management, presumably related to her female status. The characteristics themselves are drawn from stereotypic versions of genders. Yet, with this logic, Cal avoided totalizing the person as the stereotype, focusing instead on the teaching behaviors. So, while I may understand Cal's response as a quasi-sexist perspective (in contrast to women's ways of teaching), he did not see it as a male/female dichotomy or from a sexist perspective.

In contrast to the differences Cal perceived between male and female teachers, Evan was openly antagonistic toward his female colleagues. His strong excoriation of teaching, of teachers, and of education was at first offensive to me. It took me several visits and conversations to understand that his psychic distance from teaching was similar to his use of that distance to keep me away. At some point, however, we broke through that tension and arrived at a less critical way of interacting. Yet Evan's critical perspective toward teachers persisted:

> I love teaching, but I don't like teachers. I like individual teachers, but
> as a group they're a bunch of morons. Elementary teachers expect to
> be scolded for doing it [teaching] wrong. They are inadequate. (Inter-
> view, 2/22)

And lest there be any doubt that much of this criticism was directed at
women, he added "women have this job so they can have a bigger car, a
bigger house. They are working at a job." For Evan, good teaching was
about taking risks, risking to be different, standing outside the mainstream.
He was convinced that administrators are fixated on control, so there is
benefit in rewarding mediocrity and conformity. "If it says 'Do X' in the
book, [they] do it. . . . They don't reward a creative teacher. They [adminis-
trators] want people who will do what they say and who will follow" (Interview, 2/22). From Evan's perspective, men don't fit in so well in primary
grades (and elementary grades in general) because they are too autonomous
and individualistic.

In another variation on this theme, Evan offered:

> Gender is accidental. Women are attracted to little kids. Men don't
> want to play with little kids. They want to teach somebody who is
> ready to learn. Men are expected to teach high school and grown-up
> kids because it's [more] important. (Interview, 4/1)

Yet Evan did not offer to explain how it is that he is different, why his own
rules don't apply to his work with young children. My understanding is that
he did not believe what he said. It felt like he was challenging my beliefs
and trying to determine whether they matched his.

WOMEN'S TALK

The male primary teachers had a pervasive concern with their female colleagues' discourse. On one hand, female teachers' talk that accompanied
caring for their students was seen as productive. Care talk is characteristically female in education and in the larger culture. It is a discourse that
accompanies acts of caring or that supports what Noddings (1984) calls an
"ethic of care." The men saw their acquisition of care talk as an accomplishment, a problem to solve, and issue of concern. While they recognized the
difference, the male teachers simultaneously marked women's teaching talk
as special, appropriate for children, and generally something good to know
how to do. In contrast, the talk that occurred between teachers was often
devalued in gender-related ways.

Nurturing Children

For the most part, the male teachers referred to "female ways" of talking. They felt that soft and nurturing talk with young children was appropriate. With several years of primary teaching experience, Gregg suggested that children currently in his classes require a very specialized approach. When kids

> act out for attention . . . I do the soft spoken approach and give them the attention they need in a different way . . . and get the reaction that I want. They get what they need and I do, too. But I don't think they realize it. They are so used to being spoken to harshly at home, or getting a spanking. (Interview, 4/15)

Gregg recognized the students' underlying bids for attention and tried to give that attention in positive and soft-spoken ways. He contrasted this approach with the harsher methods of raised voices, threats, and physical involvement.

Similarly, Steve said, "I stop teaching to listen. I get down to their level and look at them. They know I am listening." Steve was aware of the physical behaviors in teaching that signify listening as caring. His characterization of good listening was of a receiver opening up and taking in the speaker. In contrast to producing a steady stream of talk, active listening is a constructive and creative act. Yet the use of such reflective practice may be seen as a "passive" teaching style. Gregg was also aware of the value attributed to listening and thought that it was a particular challenge for men:

> We [male teachers] need to be better listeners. We are not trained to do this. Females may be better at this learning how to listen to children. [As a result] we don't know how to find the real issues. It takes more patience to find the underlying problem. I think women handle that a little better than men do. (Interview, 4/15)

Steve admitted that "most adults (both male and female) don't know how to interact with children. I like the Ping-Pong effect rather than the one-way talk." Steve wanted reciprocity in communication, which I see as a reflection of reciprocity in relationships. When talk was with students, with children, it was productive and appropriate. However, talk between teachers was not so productive.

Interacting with Adults in School

In contrast to its special status with children, women's talk was viewed by the male participants in this study as less valued in adult contexts. An entirely different set of values was applied to primary grade teachers' discourse when that talk occurred outside of the teachers' own classrooms. During teacher meetings, goal-directed talk was seen as productive and talk about relationships as not productive. Most school meetings occur within limited timeframes, usually after school. If a group of teachers is assembled for an understood and shared purpose, then time is a limited commodity and focused talk is seen as an efficient use of that time. Gregg had given this aspect of his teaching considerable thought:

> The other men on faculty and I—we kid around—if it was an all-male faculty, we'd be out of here [a meeting] in 15 minutes and out having a beer. We don't talk about the baby showers and talk about pink snowmen on the walls. No matter what the issues [of the meeting] are, it's more of a social time [for women]. (Interview, 4/15)

When I pointed out to Gregg that he had previously spoken about how he had had to learn how to be more like the female teachers in order to be more successful with children, he responded:

> It [meeting style] had to do with who's running the school. . . . Strong principals run it like a business. You have an agenda. You go through with no tangents. Other places I've worked, the meetings are more like gripe sessions. (Interview, 4/15)

So it seemed that for Gregg, and for the majority of the participants, gender was not the issue with children because all teachers relate to children in nurturing, or "female," ways. In contrast, interpersonal and professional relationships between male and female teachers were divided along gendered lines. In speaking about "social" and "business" modes of communication, Gregg continued:

> You need both of them. We [all teachers] don't have enough time to share in our profession. So the talk sessions [social meetings] are good. And it's fun but, it is not fun if you have something to do and only a little bit of time. (Interview, 4/15)

Steve's experiences in meetings were similar to Gregg's. "In meetings, we discuss and never finalize." And in a subsequent interview, Steve reiterated,

"We never finalize. We sit and bitch and never finish. Instead of bringing up new things, we talk about the same things over and over" (Interview, 4/13).

It is important to point out that some female teachers also devalued social talk at meetings. This, of course, is no surprise when one considers an after-school meeting. Within the group, there are bound to be individuals who want to dispense with the business and head for home. According to several of the male teachers, their female colleagues were often grateful for their (the men's) efficient, focused meetings. They also agreed on characterizing others' [females'] meetings as "meandering, without agenda." And, in contrast, meetings with an agenda that stay topic-focused are good meetings.

Without Talk, with Resistance

Differences in communication styles and learning to talk with their female colleagues led to problems for several of the men. Cal doesn't want to work with his female colleagues anymore. After many years teaching third grade, he finally has an opportunity to return to his real love, kindergarten. But he will only make the switch if he can either work out a contract with the other kindergarten teachers in the pod or work on his own. He had planned to speak with a beginning female teacher about splitting the teaching responsibilities for their two classes of kindergartners. Presumably, Cal and the female teacher would split up the teaching along "gendered" subject areas. The female teacher would teach language aspects of the curriculum, and Cal would teach the more active content fields, such as mathematics, science, and social studies. Another option was that Cal would teach in a self-contained classroom. Other than a split with a single partner, Cal doesn't want an interactive set-up. "It is a problem." He had received negative feedback for his ideas and finds that other teachers, who are female, are consistently negative toward him. He thinks that other teachers cut him off in conversation because of his differences in philosophy. He has found himself less and less effective in interacting with his colleagues. "He's too far out for us," he was told. So he has concentrated on his own classroom. Cal thought that his colleagues were uninterested in discussing philosophy, history, or culture. They "turn away, turn off, don't listen." Cal's experience in teaching has been isolated, and in that solitary space he reasons that others aren't interested in what matters to him (philosophy, history, culture).

Steve also decided that isolation is a solution to avoiding misunderstandings. On one occasion, he got in trouble with his team leader for voicing his concerns about her undirected, meandering meetings. He was then confronted by her, but held his tongue. Later, he asked his other team members, all female, for their views. He determined that they agreed with him that his criticism was appropriate. Steve concluded the problem was the lead teacher's, and he decided to avoid her at lunch. "Besides," he concluded, "they talk about female things too much."

Steve's resolution may seem reasonable, but it may not be sensitive to the shifting dynamics of loyalty and confession that typify what Tannen (1990) has called "troubles talk." One of the hallmarks of this discourse is its reflexive sensitivity and reciprocity. While Steve trusted his colleagues when they talked with him supportively, they may also have offered that same supportive interaction to the team leader. From one perspective, this could be seen as a breach of trust; from another, as an argument that the participants in this discourse community may not have been using his framing for morality to constrain their talk. Steve's misogynistic discard of "female things" at the end of the previous passages is troubling because it uses female talk content as a way to disparage the talk. Yet Steve is a teacher who at other times refuses to let gendered marking affect his choices for teaching. Maybe it is harder than it appears to do so.

Trivializing Women's Talk

Communication tangles, relationship issues, and isolation were common topics for the participants. They ranged from Paul's preservice conflicts to Evan's preretirement isolation. Gregg contrasted his success with children and his difficulties with women:

> With kids I am soft-spoken, but not with adults. It bothers me that I am that way. It's not always professional. I mean, it's good to say what's on your mind, . . . [in contrast] there are a lot of people on faculty who do undercurrent things like going to someone else. I say my piece of mind. If I don't like somebody, I say so. Females talk amongst themselves when they have an issue, rather than going to the source of the issue. Men don't generally handle situations that way. If something's wrong, you go directly to the problem and try to work it out. (Interview, 4/15)

Women's "talk amongst themselves" is a curious and perhaps revealing phrase. If a female teacher is resolving an issue with another teacher, then "talk amongst themselves" would seem to be the very thing Gregg would recommend. Instead, it seems that he used the phrase to categorize and stigmatize any talking that the female teachers do together (without him). Gregg also trivialized the importance of what women teachers chose to talk about: Women "have a half-hour meeting after school to see who has the better pattern for a squirrel."

Similar to his devaluing of their trivial concerns, Gregg maintained that meetings where he wasn't the designated leader normally "just turn into gossip." The fact that people gossip is descriptive. Gregg's depiction of women's meetings as "just gossip" is something different. *Gossip* is used as a negative discourse framing, and its devalued status resides in its purported connection to women's talk. But there are other perspectives on gossip and its uses.

Spacks's (1985) analysis of gossip suggests an alternative. "This excitement [of gossip] includes the heady experience of imaginative control: gossip claims other people's experience by interpreting it into a story" (p. 11). Of course, a story can be critiqued as a fiction and, therefore, not true. Spacks goes on to problematize her own fascination with gossip. "Anyone can gossip. People like to do so because they achieve an effortless illusion of understanding" (p. 17). Not unlike Woods's (1987) critique of Nias's (1985) reference groups for primary teachers, Spacks suggests that "understanding" is illusory. Teachers may be viewed as creating community with a surface of understanding through our mutual sharing of what Tannen (1990) calls "small secrets." According to this view, gossip functions as a transactional medium, and relationships are built through the give and take of small secrets. Perhaps the construction of teaching competence, or at least the shared perception that such competence is possessed, is built on short transactions of teaching talk, analogous to Tannen's "troubles talk." Then competence is an attribute that is mediated by ability to talk about it. Isolated teachers, like Fred, Evan, and Cal, can thus be seen as less competent by others who may gossip about them.

DISCIPLINE

When parents, principals, and teachers suggest that students need a male teacher, the issues are often ones of discipline and control. The assumption, which is usually unexamined, is that men as teachers are somehow better able to provide problem students with discipline. Buried beneath these beliefs are notions about gender roles, about teaching, and about how they map onto each other. A male teacher is somehow predisposed to be better at discipline. By default, female teachers are less able to provide appropriate discipline. These assumptions are made without regard to what is meant by discipline and what kind of teaching behaviors would be more likely to facilitate productive discipline. Rather, the preceding relationship drawn between men and discipline adopts an authoritarian and external approach without critical examination.

Another issue is the construction of discipline as a practice equated with a male vision of social conduct in schools. The enactment of effective discipline based on male versions of reality could, in fact, elicit the very behaviors that must be "disciplined." This kind of teaching can involve demonstrations of physical strength, volume and timbre in voice, social distance, and competition. Often, when I hear "We need more men in elementary . . ." I shudder to think what "they" need us for. In discussing maleness as a prerequisite for discipline, the males who taught in the primary grades were also concerned about other adults' and children's expectations for "the man teacher's" behavior.

Failing to Discipline

Fred's first year of teaching was one of despair. He understood this "disastrous year" as a "problem with discipline." Like any personal difficulty, this one came with many layers. All the difficult students were assigned to Fred's room, because, in his words, "I'm a male." As the newest first-grade teacher, he did not have a classroom until his "portable" arrived in October. Until that time, he functioned as a teacher's aide for the other, female first-grade teachers. His eventual class of students had previously been distributed among the other teachers. At the beginning of the year, Fred met with small groups of students on the fringes of his colleagues' classrooms. When his portable classroom was trucked in, Fred, now familiar with the students in the whole of the first grade, looked at his new class and realized that he had been "dumped on." In his group of children, he found the "problem students" from all of his colleagues' classes.

Further complicating the situation was his students' perception of Fred as an aide to other teachers. If Fred was a teacher's aide, he was presumably subordinate to their "real teachers." He told me he was not ready for such a hard test and was angry with the other teachers for an unsupported initiation. In a portable, he was isolated from the other teachers and from any help that might have made things better. He suggested that the qualities that got him a job were his competence, confidence, and independence—the very ones that worked against his getting help when his classroom teaching "went bad."

> I came across as clean-cut, very professional, very competent. I had a lot of options for where I wanted to teach. I had schools calling me asking "Are you hired?" even after I took a job here. (Interview, 2/17)

In this first year of teaching, Fred had several relational issues with members of this unruly class. However, because he did not socialize with the other teachers, he was not aware of services and support that were available. Fred saw his isolation as part of a choice. Rather than participate in what he saw as talk that didn't involve him, he stuck to himself. But on his own, and without the mentoring that social connection would have provided, he struggled through a difficult first year. Fred understood his "initiation" as "hazing" related to the fact that he is male. He characterized the year as "being squeezed out, not being part of school . . . it seems to happen . . . I spend a lot of time by myself. I do it to myself, sort of a cover. I don't go out of my way to meet people. I eat in my room" (Interview, 2/17). Without connection to others, in isolation, Fred was forced to go it alone.

> I had been initiated. I felt angry at the administration. "You should be able to handle these kids." She [the assistant principal] didn't understand my teaching situation. I can't do anything cute. These are streetwise first-graders. (Interview, 2/17)

In an interview at the end of the school year, Fred looked exhausted. He commented on his first year: "It was horrible. I'm beat. It's horrible reliving it. Towards the end, my self esteem came up, my teaching took a turn" (Interview, 6/2). He related his teaching turn-around to two events. The first was the removal of a severely disturbed student from his class. The second was a turn inward and the discovery that this first-grade class was his "last stop." Because he had already made one career change, he felt compelled to succeed in teaching. Somehow he found the strength to become "the teacher" in his class.

A condition that precipitated his nightmarish experience was the school's construction of Fred as *the* disciplinarian for the other (female) first-grade teachers. As a result of this unstated role assignment, Fred's involvement with discipline was so complete and so all-consuming that he couldn't do anything productive with this atypical group of first-graders. If Fred had been a female teacher, he would have been allowed to need help and receive support for his teaching. Yet it would have been problematic to help the disciplinarian. Men are less permitted to need help. Reliving his induction year in our interviews, he dramatized: "It was awful! 'You have to take my bad kids. You're a man. You can handle it.' I don't want to handle it. I don't want to handle anything that you don't handle!" (Interview, 6/5). Fred was visibly agitated and struggled for composure. As he let go in anger, some of the pressure from his first year escaped. Not allowed to need help, and isolated in a portable classroom, Fred festered until outsiders could no longer ignore it and only then intervened. Now he is working to repair himself, his teaching and his ego, to get ready for his second year as a first-grade teacher.

Resisting the Call to Discipline

Steve was told that he was given a certain child because he was a man and the child needed a male figure. He understood this as an implied request for stricter, harsher discipline. His dramatized response was: "Why did you give him to me? Why don't you give him to her or to her?" He didn't feel that he was any different from a neighbor teacher and saw the action as sexist. The issue of men's responsibility for discipline common to all the participants. Their reactions were often to be resentful, angry, and hurt. The male primary teachers in the study resisted the "male as disciplinarian" on philosophical grounds. As Gregg reasoned, "Discipline is inside the kids. It's definitely not something outside your own classroom." More pragmatically, relying on the male teacher was seen as an unfair, unprofessional practice. The approach of progressive, child-centered teachers of young children, such as Gregg, is to shift from control by the teacher to an internalized control in the mind of the child. Locating discipline is complex. Walkerdine (1990) acknowledges that from progressive views, discipline resides inside the child. This is similar to Gregg's statements about his discipline beliefs. Yet, Walkerdine also points out that in arranging for young students' self-regulation, teachers, who are usually female, must remove themselves from the picture to make room for the self-regulating child. For Walkerdine, it is an issue of some consequence for female teachers. From my perspective, this self-displacement is a different phenomenon for male teachers.

Steve's construction of discipline appears to be that individual teachers are responsible for maintaining order when they are in charge of a group of children. Regarding disciplining his class for special subjects, he added:

> How "specials" see my class is important. When my kids are with me, they're OK. It's like they're "show dogs." If they do misbehave in art, music, or PE, that's that teacher's problem. [But] they [special-subject teachers] won't even fill out an accident report. (Interview, 4/13)

Steve saw discipline as something that has qualities, such as respect, order, and awareness of others, and is transferable from one situation to another. It is something that can be managed by different people when they are in charge of the children. So the adult is not even the whole issue. Discipline is about the development of competencies within the children. Yet, while discipline is tacitly embedded in a relationship between the teacher and student, it is necessary that teachers share the construction of discipline as a context for a given child. When special-subject teachers refuse "to even fill out accident reports," Steve implicates them for not taking part in managing students' behavior.

Steve also viewed discipline as situationally grounded. An individual situation might require "discipline" that is quite different from that used in other situations. There seems to be a balance between the students and the teachers in the construction of discipline. In any case, discipline is not something that anyone else can do for us when we are "the teacher." In his view, a female teacher might complain to other teachers, male and female, about her kids, with the implicit expectation that the second teacher would assume some of the problem. For Steve, discipline belongs to the teacher who is in charge of the students.

Steve's understanding of discipline as an individual teacher's construction would have precluded him from helping Fred regain control of his classroom. Here are two different approaches to establishing an orderly classroom. Fred, who needed help during his first year, unsuccessfully continued alone. Steve, who was successful with his class discipline, looked for teachers of special subjects to take responsibility for their share of the management of behavior.

Problems with Discipline

Gregg believed that teachers' perspectives on discipline, order, and control change with as they mature and gain additional experience with teaching. Teachers come to know more about what they can do. And with more discerning knowledge comes the ability to choose issues of control more carefully. Gregg recognized that the children he has taught in recent years are more aggressive in their bids for attention. He was reluctant to act out himself and try to control them in aggressive (male) ways. He relates: "Some of my more recent kids act out for attention. So, I do the "poppa-bit," the soft-spoken approach, and give them the attention that they need in a different way. . . . I don't see harsh discipline working" (Interview, 4/15). Gregg spoke softly in the interview as well. I can't imagine him getting angry or raising his voice in his classroom. Yet he acknowledged that he does raise his voice sometimes when children fail to respond. When he has run out of understanding and options, he sends the second-grade offenders to time-out.

With an organized and reasonable approach to managing children in a classroom, men are at risk for being attributed these skills simply because they are men. Much like the paradox female teachers face as "natural-born caregivers," men teachers face similar issues when they are seen as "natural-born disciplinarians."

When Gregg began teaching, he remembered being snared by the expectation that he "could control kids," not just his, but all of them. "I used to think I should or could solve all the problems." He thought that he, as well as other men in primary grades, have had to contend with a "hero complex." He believed his early difficulties with teaching, which caused him to leave teaching for 12 years, had to do with his perception of himself as the one who had to take care of everything. Now he has a different understanding of how far his responsibilities extend. Others can and do take over at his personal limits. Men, from my perspective, are expected to be independent problem solvers from our childhood days. In fact, women who are independent individuals stand out in schools. In a context where almost all participants are female, nurturing, and raised to listen to what men tell them, it is likely that men who enter this environment will reproduce relationships learned in the broader culture. To the extent that these examples are prototypes for other interactions, these males who teach in primary grades seem uniform in resisting the seduction of disciplining others' students.

For me, the call to discipline is related to the privilege male primary teachers experience as the local representatives of the patriarchy. Often the male teacher in elementary schools is the only professional male in the building. Other men may work in the building as custodians and grounds-keepers, but they are usually not eligible for discipline duties because of lower social status. However, I do remember my fifth-grade classmate, Joe, who was repeatedly sent to the boiler room to sit with Mr. Costas, the "maintenance man." It is hard to imagine that Mr. Costas was any more intimidating than was Sister Camilla.

So, male primary teachers' refusal to discipline reneges on the patriarchal bargain struck in the larger culture. It is interesting to consider how their refusal relates to perceptions of authority, deference, and allocation of participation structures in faculty groups. At its most extreme, discipline is about physically hurting children to establish consequences for their undesirable (or lack of desirable) behavior.

GENDER AND TEACHING: A SUMMARY

Using gender as a lens through which to view male primary teachers' work establishes a related set of comparisons between male and females who work in this teaching world. According to the men in the study, gender is not as important as the impact of the teaching behavior, regardless of how it may signify as gender. This was true for the teachers' behavior with children. Yet, in their interactions with colleagues, the male primary teachers understood themselves as different from their colleagues. They systematically devalued women's teaching and nonteaching behaviors to establish themselves as different, and women as other. The frames of difference that they used were texts, curricula, discipline, and talk. Like care, gender is at once ambiguous and contingent. Gender is less salient in interactions with students, where teacher behaviors are evaluated vis-à-vis their productivity with children. In contrast, interactions with other adults were seen as opportunities to establish themselves as male in contrast to female, a state that was seen as a problem.

Men's refusal to respond to female colleagues' requests for discipline was a particularly complex transaction. On the one hand, the men can be seen resisting other teachers' requests for what might be inappropriate practices from a child-centered perspective. On the other hand, such a refusal also exempts the men from playing their part in a patriarchal economy of relations, where women care and men discipline.

In addition, ability and inability to communicate within women's ways of talking had important effects on their effectiveness and satisfaction with teaching, particularly outside their own classrooms. One participant, Ken, claimed a direct relationship between his sexual orientation and his ability to communicate in women's ways. Of course, all such connections drawn between sexual orientation and teaching are not so direct or positive. The following chapter examines how sexualities have been used as part of teaching.

CHAPTER 12

Permissible Teachers: Desire and Sexual Orientations

"People think you're gay because you're in [primary] education." Steve's comment isolates what many of the male primary teachers mentioned. They reported that their sexual orientations were common themes in the ways others understood men's roles in primary education. It is a problematic assumption for several reasons. First of all, to claim that certain men are or are not gay is a discussion based on the privileges of heterosexuality and its separation from other sexualities. Ethically, this is any person's private business. Logically, the question is irrelevant. Since teachers' sexual lives are not explicitly part of their teaching lives, asking the question is not congruent with professional definitions of a teacher. The question itself becomes suspect, and the suspicion centers on men's sexual potentialities. However, statistically, instances of child sexual abuse are most often committed across genders, by men who identify themselves as heterosexuals, and usually within family settings (Batchelor, Dean, Gridley, & Batchelor, 1990; Finkelhor, Williams, & Burns, 1988; Tricket & Susman, 1988). Politically, speculation about the sexual orientation of men who intend to teach in the primary grades is often used to dissuade, manipulate, and select men, gay and heterosexual, who work in primary grade classrooms. This chapter examines some of the issues of sexual orientations, life partners, effeminacy, and perceived suitability as they impinged on these men who taught in the primary grades.

TEACHERS AND SEXUAL ORIENTATIONS

The preceding arguments to the contrary, sexual orientation, or more specifically, the teachers' presumptions about others' beliefs about the their (the teachers') sexual orientations, was an important issue for the men who taught in the primary grades. One such social construction, the "gay primary teacher," worked in at least two ways in this study. First, the responses from

107

the men in the study who self-identified as gay were typically that teachers' sexual orientation, gay *or* straight, was irrelevant, since their teaching was not related to their sexuality. Ken's self-representation, both in Chapter 6 and here, is illustrative. Second, responses from the men in the study who self-identified as heterosexual were typically about denial of others' attributions of homosexuality. Steve's remarks from Chapter 5, reinstated here with others' experiences, are presented as examples of how orientation extortion worked to control all male teachers' behaviors.

Separate and Unequal Lives

As Ken, a gay kindergarten teacher, put it, "The issue of being gay has nothing to do with the kids. It's more about the fear of adult reprisals." Ken told me that his principal, some other teachers, and even district-level administrators "knew" that he was gay. "But no one," Ken added, "talked about it. We use veiled language and reference my outside-of-school life obliquely." Even in this discussion, Ken added to the euphemisms that represent his "outside-of-school life." These are compelling habits and effective survival language. Ken's life is often one of parallel language and dichotomized social realities.

Ken related that his separate, gay life became part of his daily teaching life out of necessity. As he described in Chapter 6, his partner of several years, Gary, became progressively more incapacitated as AIDS ravaged his body. Ken was his primary care provider and was torn between caring for his kindergartners and caring for his life partner. Ken's life was suddenly centered on one person, in one room, of one hospital. He returned to his classroom at intervals. His leave from teaching was acknowledged and approved by his principal, aided and abetted by his friend and classroom aide, and understood and supported by his teaching colleagues. Ken says everybody knew what was going on. "How could they not know? I showed up intermittently looking like a zombie!"

Yet throughout the slow death of his partner, Ken never named his partner's illness or explicitly shared any information that would have made the principal aware of Ken's circumstances. He surmised that if she officially "knew" of his involvement in extended AIDS care, she would have been compelled to alert others in the chain of school authority. With naming and official knowledge of categorized and negatively marked behavior, Ken's job would have been at risk.

Ken talked about his deceased partner and his second, current partner and the demands his teaching makes on his personal life.

Both of my partners have been real good at becoming invisible. At K-Mart, I'll say, "There's Mrs. Smith. I taught Johnny two years ago." I look back to introduce Jack to Mrs. Smith, and the cart is gone and him with it. (Interview, 2/17)

Keeping his personal life separate from his professional life was an accommodation that seemed to work in some situations, like a chance meeting with parents. Yet, even there, I am left to wonder about what the parent thought about Jack's disappearance. His disappearance and Ken's discomfort may have induced parents to wonder "Is it shame?" "Is it me?" I also wonder about the vibrations it would set up inside Ken and Jack's relationship. Separation of his "lives" seemed to Ken at other times to be a burden:

> To keep them separate is not natural. The hardest part is when I'm with co-workers. They say something about their husbands and something similar has happened to me. I can't say "Oh yeah, Jack . . . " It would be educating them, bridging the gap between the gay and straight worlds. But I'd get the feeling that I was pushing my agenda, taking every opportunity to cram it down their throats. I've gotten this feedback from my friends—that all I was talking about was my homosexuality [as a condition]. They talk about their lives, but when we [gay men] do, we are talking about our "lifestyle." Everybody wants to talk about their lives. (Interview, 2/17)

While Ken talked freely with me about his gay life, he was animated and entertaining; hours passed. Suddenly, he stopped to check his anonymity and asked whether or not the people at work could read this and be able to identify him. His abrupt monitoring took him to a story about two other gay male teachers in his elementary building. They had the same planning period while their students were in special subjects and were going to lunch together. The sixth-graders noticed them together and started rumors that the teachers were kissing and holding hands. The students took the rumors home. A parent let a female teacher at the school site know what was being talked about in the community. The female teacher suggested to the two men that they reconsider how they behaved in public. To Ken's knowledge, there was no romantic involvement between the two men, one of whom is half of a couple in a committed relationship.

Ken remembered his early years of teaching as ones during which he was "really closeted":

> I just knew that the superintendent would be waiting on the other side of the door [to a gay bar] ready to tear up my teaching certificate. The first time I went to a gay bar, the world didn't end, so I went to happy hour—every week. And within a year of coming out, I was in my first relationship. (Interview 2/17)

Ken's committed relationship raises an important paradox for men that emerged in our discussions. Men who are married to women and who teach in primary grades are often seen as "less suspect." They are presumably not gay, and, more important, they become less threatening sexually when they have committed to a marriage. A parallel argument can be made for gay men who are in committed relationships with other men. They are no longer available as sexual partners and should be sexually less threatening in the school context. From my perspective, men's sexuality, relative to women's, *is* more autonomous and articulated in the culture as more active and aggressive. I see this as a significant impediment to overcome. However, the paradox we experience as gay men in relationships is that our own lives with a partner project us into even higher relief as a "gay couple." With the purposeful representation of "gay" in the context of a relationship, we are less able to, and in my case less willing to, live marginalized lives that permit only liminal representation of important aspects of who we are. But the category "gay" is even more sexually circumscribed than that of "male."

Both Ken and I "came out" as gay men late in our lives and well into our established professional identities. In some ways, that has provided both of us with some personal security and confidence. In other contexts, such as in our communities, Ken and I both have a certain outspokenness and politicized relationship to our sexual orientations and to our teaching. I understand Ken's complaint about the trap of self-representation. Sexual orientation, locating the object of sexual desire, is not a matter of choice. Engaging with the social world as a "gay man" is a choice. Both from the interviews and from our friendship, I know that he is much more complex than a label of "gay male" on his forehead.

Being Gay Is Being Like a Woman

Accusations of being gay are also used as epithets against straight men who choose to teach primary grades. Such labeling is intended to intimidate. Steve's encounters with this bullying were illustrative. In the following excerpt, he recalled a conversation from college and reflected on its effects:

> "People think you're gay because you're in education." "Who said that?" "Oh, just some people. And I told them you were." "Oh, well thank-you." [with heavy sarcasm] I don't know, I guess hanging around a bunch of women and doing artsy craftsy things. (Interview, 4/13)

Steve denied that he is gay but not the underlying assumptions that put him "at risk." He did not directly question the belief that gay men characteristically do "female things." As pointed out earlier, he did argue that men have the right to do things that are identified as female and that doing so should not carry social sanction. He continued:

> I was fine in college. I was in a fraternity and all that. It's just the snide little comments. . . . Maybe people think that only women can teach, be caregivers. And if you are acting like that, maybe you're gay. (Interview, 4/13)

In Steve's example, acting like a woman signified being gay. However, this time it was others who were making the connection, perhaps mistakenly from Steve's perspective. He did think that some men were dissuaded from elementary education, especially in the primary grades, because "they are afraid of their feminine side." As we talked, he assumed the character of the ambivalent male, trying to decide whether or not to be a teacher. "Maybe they'll think I'm weird or maybe they'll think I'm gay." Now, feminine, weird, and gay were all brought to the same side of the analysis. In choosing a character, Steve did not own these values but saw them in others. Steve's fears were not unique; his awareness and ability to articulate his beliefs were. He reasoned:

> Had I not been married and had begun teaching, there would be questions. That's the mentality. . . . When I started teaching, I carefully placed a picture of my wife on my desk. What difference does it make? When I was single and interning, the parents came to check me out. I think what they're afraid of is that I'm gay . . . [and] that if someone is gay they're a child molester. (Interview, 5/7)

Steve didn't believe in the chain of logic he had just created, but he knew it to exist. He summarized: "What difference does it make? Women can be gay. Men can be gay. But as long as they are providing care for kids . . . " (Interview, 5/7).

I agree. But living under the threat that one shouldn't be gay, be like a women, is oppression that exacts costs. Steve reacted with purposeful behavior, rather like his purposeful and strategic use of female behaviors that were functionally related to teaching. Placing a picture of his wife on his desk was a gesture. The fact that he connected it with a purpose made it a strategy for fending off others' speculations about his sexual orientation. This is accommodating to oppression.

Steve's resistance brings to the surface one of the differences between gay and straight men in the study. The three gay men characteristically confronted the underlying assumptions when others conflated gay and male primary teacher. In conversation with me they would agree with the stereotypic accusation, that they were gay. Yet the agreement was a surface response with resistance as a subtext. The gay men contested the association as a necessarily negative one (1) by asserting that there was no association between sexual orientation and teaching competence and (2) by suggesting, as Ken did, that his teaching competence was enhanced by his orientation. There is a subtle distinction to be made here. My understanding of Ken's argument is for the inclusion and valuing of his social performance of himself as a gay man. That is, his acquired expertise with women's ways of knowing, caring, connecting, and teaching, all thought to enhance his teaching, were related to his prior experiences as a gay male in the company of women.

For the men who did not identify themselves as gay, the dynamics of resistance were different. Each of the heterosexual men who discussed others' accusations was careful to state that he was "not gay, but why even bring it up" because the comparison was irrelevant.

Disclosure and Self-Representation

For self-identified gay men who teach young children, the stakes are much higher. Today in Florida, there is overt pressure to "out" gay and lesbian teachers so that they can be forced out of their teaching positions. The gay teachers in this study may lose their jobs. The internal binary of self-worth and pride contrasted with hiding and secrecy are everyday realities for gay primary teachers. Ken claimed he simply couldn't talk freely about his life partner. Yet he consciously pushes himself to be as open as he can in each social circumstance.

> When Gary [Ken's first partner] died, I went to a Gay Pride celebration . . . that kind of radicalized me. . . . Usually when I do talk about Jack [Ken's second, current partner], I say "we" and I never really define the other part of "we." I feel as though my co-workers must feel as though they've walked in on the middle of a movie. (Interview, 4/5)

Ken also claimed a relationship among his gayness, his childhood, and his teaching. He concurred with another participant, Cal, that primary education is a highly verbal and female context. Yet, unlike Cal, Ken sought to be a practicing member of the local norms. In talking about gay men, he said, "We're verbal because we hung out in the kitchen." This makes sense to me because I hung out in the kitchen. It fits, in a glib way, how I understand coming to know what I know about women's ways of talking. But I am also aware of many gay friends, some of whom are primary teachers, whom I would consider quiet and reserved.

Because of repeated experiences in women's company, such as choosing the kitchen over football in the living room, Ken is comfortable working with women. He suggests that "men [gay and heterosexual] who choose to work in a female context and not work within women's ways of knowing do so with some costs." Here, Ken referred to the "lone wolves" he had defined earlier, men who choose to stick to themselves in elementary school culture. However, Ken did not see these choices as being made along lines of gender or lines of sexual orientation. Rather, it is the ability—however acquired, however understood—to work with children and other teachers within women's ways of knowing. Ken related that he has worked with several men who identify themselves as heterosexual and who are also very effeminate. He suggested that these are "straight men who know women's ways." Ken understood his own positioning in line with this statement and personalized it with:

> I think I'm good because I overcompensate. I know people will be looking at me. . . . Number one, because I'm male. Number two, because they suspect that I'm gay. And if they are going to be looking, they're going to looking at something good. (Interview, 4/5)

Indeed, Ken's gambit seemed to be working. He was consistently profiled in the local newspaper ("the gentle giant") whenever a "good example" of a male teacher of young children was wanted. True to form, he was aware of the "use" potential in such representation, and he turned it to his advantage. "At least if they're the stories they [newspaper] talk about, it gives them something positive."

The men who participated in this study had varying levels of comfort with their acquired status of "potential homosexuals." Their comfort levels were not contingent on their self-identified sexual orientations. Some of the gay teachers in the study, like Ken, did not feel particularly threatened by others' speculation. Others, like Fred, felt very threatened. Similarly, the teachers who identified themselves as heterosexuals varied in their comfort levels and accommodation strategies to others' speculations.

From my perspective, two factors that affected participants' comfort levels with others' speculation were age and number of years teaching. The older participants, both gay and straight, seemed to have some understanding of their situation. Younger informants, such as Steve and Fred, seemed more concerned. The number of years spent teaching also seemed to have a relationship with comfort levels. While these factors certainly have some overlap, two of the participants suggest discrete effects as well. Van was in his 40s during the study, but completing his first year of teaching. He was reflective about the risk of being seen as potentially gay and potentially pedophilic. "It's part of the job," he refrained. Fred was a younger beginning teacher who was concerned about his self-representation as a gay man. At 25 years old, Steve was in his third year of teaching and very concerned about others' perceptions of his sexual persona. Overall, the orientations were not the motivation for anxiety. But the anxiety, greater for younger and less experienced teachers, was certainly there for all the teachers.

Coping strategies notwithstanding, it is necessary to understand the rationale behind the use of these unethical bullying tactics. To do so requires a return to the idea that teaching in the primary grades is a profession of caring.

HISTORICAL (DIS)PLACEMENT OF TEACHERS

As previously noted, teaching in the primary grades has been considered "women's work." The professional personnel for that work have also been influenced by patriarchal constructions of "women who work" (with children). Until the 1930s, female teachers in many areas were expected to be virgins. They were often required to be single and were not allowed to date. When they married, they left teaching. Later, when marriage was allowed, pregnant women were forced out of teaching. Essentially, the regulations that selected who would be allowed to teach defined a slot where only chaste women fit.

To teach, women were required to lack sexuality. A remnant from the social mores of Victorian sexual repression, female teachers were expected to represent themselves as having no sexuality. This repression is related to a Western morality that split caring from sexuality. One could not be nurturing *and* sexual, since Eros was the feared demon that, if not constrained, would overwhelm the goodness of a caring relationship with base and evil sex. Such reasoning appears quaint, perhaps repressive, in retrospect. But the effect of these historical limitations on teachers lingers in our current concepts of "teacher." Our individual constructions of the ideal teacher contain vestiges of these attributes and ultimately control current-day teachers. It is important to understand the effects of these liminal dynamics on the teachers in this study and the explanatory power of these embedded expectations for the findings in this study. Consider the following ubiquitous effect.

One can see the problem in combining the categories of "gay" and "teacher," whether or not such categorizing is based on fact. In popular culture, gay men are defined by sexual difference (cf. Browning, 1993, for an interesting discussion of the queer culture perspective). By extension of that perceived difference, gay men are often construed as "oversexed" and/

or as sexuality turned bad or evil. In this sense, a gay man may be seen as the opposite of the chaste woman American culture wanted (wants?) teaching its children. In the 1930s Waller wrote:

> The real danger is that [a homosexual man] *may*, by presenting himself as a love object to certain members of his own sex at a time when their sex attitudes have not been deeply canalized, develop in them attitudes similar to his own. For nothing seems more certain than that homosexuality is contagious. (1932, pp. 147–148; emphasis added)

Waller's belief that one's sexual orientation is subject to conditioning is now largely discredited in the medical and psychological communities (LeVay, 1996). Moreover, recent writing points out that same-sex relationships as well as their systematic misrepresentation have been present throughout history (Boswell, 1984, 1994). The bigotry that informed such purposefully inaccurate representation of same-sex couples and couplings persists. And teachers, both gay and heterosexual, continue to deal with the tenacious fallout from the sexual regulations of earlier times (King, 1997). At least Waller conditioned his argument with *may*. Current accusations against a male who teaches young children may not be so careful. However, it is also important to point out that these social constructions about groups of people are essentially not accurate, as the following arguments make clear.

The Costs of Caring Covertly

The perception that men who teach in primary grades and in preschools are homosexuals is entangled with the perception that homosexual males are effeminate. The combination of these largely inaccurate perceptions of homosexuality, teaching, and gendered behavior has had a disastrous effect on teachers. As a closeted, gay primary teacher, I constantly monitored my behaviors around children. I was anxious about how other teachers, parents, and principals would interpret my interactions and relationships with my students. The paradox that my self-monitoring engendered is complex. As a strong child advocate, I value the concern that I and other adults had and have for children. Therefore, like others around me, I was and am careful about the influences that prevail among the children I teach. Yet how can I, by virtue of my sexual orientation, be unhealthy for kids? Because I was aware that others believed social contact with homosexuals to be harmful for children, I monitored myself carefully.

It is important to point out the contradictions inherent in these assertions. I am not suggesting that teachers should not monitor their behavior around children. Adult interpretations of experience are not always appropriate for young children, either in and out of school. This is particularly true in power-based social relations in which adults typically hold the power. But when the motive for monitoring is for a performance of who I am as a person, when the underlying category for the behavior is unrelated to teaching, I must take issue. It is also important to point out that some male teachers in the primary grades are gay; and some men, gay and nongay, are effeminate. But the relationship of these categories to teaching and to each other is ambiguous and flexible. When they become fixed by others, it is usually with regulative intent (King, 1997).

As a classroom teacher, I internalized the monitoring of my homosexuality that I imagined others were doing. I remember deciding what to say to other teachers, whom I should sit with at lunch, how artistic I could be with classroom decor, and how I would justify so many plants on the old oak windowsills of my fifth-grade classroom. Self-monitoring was also a ubiquitous part of my self-representation to my students. Like Ken, when I saw any of my students in K-Mart with their families, I was often embarrassed because I was certain they could tell I was gay. I felt my face flush and had the sensation of being trapped. I now understand that my own homophobia had much to do with my fear that the parents had "figured me out." In monitoring my embarrassment and in checking to see if I had let anything slip, I created and collected the data for my own self-hatred. So while I support the need to be scrupulous about who influences our children, I think that the automatic suspicion of gay men is something quite different. Further, the use of "gay" to discredit all men in primary teaching is something else, also different in intent.

Rofes (1985) presents a compelling portrait of his struggles as a closeted, gay elementary teacher. He endured successive stages of self-representation in his constant struggle to have an integrated life. He ultimately left teaching, frustrated that he could not simultaneously be gay and a teacher. But his decision to leave teaching was not based on any conflict between his sexual desires and his behavior toward his students. Rather, it was based on his frustrations about fragmenting his life, personal guilt about dishonesty, and fear that his self-representation as a gay man would reduce his teaching effectiveness. Nias's (1989) description of "feeling like a [primary] teacher" hinges on themes of "being yourself," "being whole," "being natural," and "establishing relationships with children" (pp. 181–186). Likewise, Noddings's (1984) dictum that teachers "be totally and nonselectively present to the student" (p. 180) presents a problem for teachers who are already vested in selective disclosure of who they "really are."

I do not read Noddings as advocating, nor am I arguing for, teachers' (gay and straight) rights to be sexual with children. Rather, teachers have a right to represent themselves, including their sexual orientations. Nor do I suggest that gay and lesbian teachers should discuss their private lives in ways different from heterosexual teachers. The important point about gay teachers' freedom for self-representation is a release from the internalized paranoia and self-loathing that can prevent us from "being there" for children. Of course, to do so can be very difficult when gay teachers feel threatened to be themselves.

Four of the participants in this study (including myself) were self-identified gay men. My experience in teaching suggests that we were not an atypical group. Yet my intent is not to categorize primary teachers, male or female, in any configuration. The point is that if teachers, gay or straight, must spend their psychic energy concealing their "substantial selves" (Nias, 1989), then they are less available for their (our) work with children.

Sexuality and the Performance of School Identities

Feeling paranoid about our sexual orientation, gay and lesbian teachers have adopted coping strategies that, in my opinion, reduce our effectiveness as teachers. In an interview study of British gay and lesbian teachers, Squirrel (1989) describes closeted gay teachers trying "to pass" as nongay. With students, the teachers ducked answers to questions that related to their gay lives. They were also secretive about their lives outside of school. They physically and psychologically distanced themselves from their students in an effort to conceal their sexual orientations. While some would argue that teachers, in general, *should* separate home and school lives, my own perception is that such separation is difficult, taxing, and fragmenting. It is costly for teachers and reduces their relationship with their students. Separation, distance, and lack of self-disclosure are the conditions in teaching that Noddings (1984, 1992) has argued against. These conditions are certainly unlike what Nias (1989) has described as typical for primary (elementary) teachers in Britain. And a further consideration is the issue of whether or not a teacher will choose to segregate home and school. Gay men and lesbians don't usually choose to be closeted. And to suggest that *only* gay and lesbian teachers should conceal their lives lived outside of school is an example of the discrimination that gay and lesbian teachers are working to reveal and overturn.

Working from a cultural assumption that homosexuality is inappropriate, the teachers in Squirrel's (1989) study struggled with the "inappropriateness of revealing their own sexuality" (p. 101). Lesbian teachers chose not to speak up with the understanding that when speaking as lesbians their words would discredit the cause for which they spoke. The self-criticism inherent in such positioning is both painful and understandable. Gay men reported creating a facade of heterosexuality. They frequently had special female friends who would pose as partners.

Squirrel (1989) suggests that an underlying homophobic assumption in the culture is that gay teachers will recruit young boys into homosexual lifestyles—an assumption that exacts very serious costs. Its impact is pervasive. Despite its ludicrousness, my awareness of this assumption influences my work with students. A colleague who observed my teaching for a semester (King & Holland, 1992) noted that my "style" of teaching included much one-on-one conferencing and frequent use of "casual touch." In a debriefing she pointed out that I did not interact this way with Chris, a tall, blond, handsome undergraduate. I quickly pointed out that I felt unsafe teaching young males in my classes. I figured that they knew I was gay. She pointed out, equally quickly, that I seemed to have no reservations in tete-à-tete's with, and in physically touching, Justin. Margaret had already hypothesized and verified what was now dawning on me. Justin was large, overweight, participatory, and unattractive (to me).

I use this example to teach myself. The big lesson is that even when I think I know what I'm doing, I don't. I can't know all the things that I am doing, because each participant has a different take on "what's going on here?" I think Chris was afforded a very different course and learning experience when I closed myself off to interaction with him. To have based my teaching decisions on students' physical attractiveness and my fantasmic, internalized desire for them is not a teaching approach that I wish to maintain. I think that the misrepresentation that I allowed myself is more possible in a repressed state of denial about my desire. I am not unique in this regard.

There are countless examples of self-monitoring and self-censoring based on my sexual orientation and quasi-sexual desire that affect my caring relationships with my students, both male and female. The point here is that orientation itself is not the issue. It is how professionals in educational contexts deal with their desire. I think recognition is healthier than denial. Denial does not eradicate the desire. Why, then, do others fixate on the sexual orientation of male teachers?

Gay Teachers and Work Differentiation

The fact that sexual orientation is used to control access to teaching is related to a cultural and economic use of "homosexuality." Homosexuality is a relatively new construct (Foucault, 1978). It is an invention of the twentieth century created for political and economic control of people, especially men.

Following the arguments of Foucault (1978) and Sedgwick (1985), Owens (1992) reasons that homophobia is a ritualized mechanism of social control. Owens suggests that there is great utility in viewing homosexual men as outsiders, or others. Then, given the public perception that all men are, or should be, heterosexual, they can be manipulated with accusations of homosexuality. The success of using sexual orientation as a lever for social control depends on creating and intensifying the criminality as well as the feminization of homosexuality. While such homophobic practices are most certainly oppressive to women and gay men, Owens suggests that their more pervasive influences are in regulating the behavior of *all* men. "The imputing of homosexual motive to every male relationship is thus 'an immensely potent tool . . . for manipulation of every form of power that [is] refracted through the gender system—that is, in European society, of virtually every form of power' (Sedgwick, pp. 88–89)" (p. 221). I would also reinforce the obvious but no less significant point that homophobic social control invests heavily in misogynistic practice by "feminizing" homosexuality in order to devalue it.

The same arguments can be mapped onto the gatekeeping that restricts men's participation in primary education. These hegemonic practices appropriate females' cultural space, in this case primary education, with the intent to devalue males' work in that space. Men's dominance in a patriarchal economic system and women's subordinate work are preserved. In addition, the gatekeeping that occurs at the entrance to primary teaching also appropriates the cultural space of homosexual men. The hidden message to men who choose to teach primary grades is that "those teachers are usually homosexual." And given the undesirability of homosexuality, men may be dissuaded from teaching in the early grades.

GENDER, SEXUALITY, AND SCHOOL TALK

Can we talk about sex? The answer is no. Not in schools. And especially not in the primary grades. And don't even think about sex if you happen to be gay. It is not surprising that the talk surrounding men, sexuality, and children is quiet, and whispered. Yet the evidence is everywhere. Our fingers cover our lips as we whisper about Mr. So and So. Our eyes flick from side to side as we monitor our eavesdroppers. And our pulses quicken, our breathing becomes shallow, and stomachs knot, wondering about Mr. So and So and our lunches with him for 3 years. We know with our bodies that this is the talk that can end careers and send people to jail as well as make for a juicy story. Yet the topic is cloaked in silence.

Silence and Desire

Fine (1987, 1992) has written convincingly about the role of silence in schools. Fine's (1987) essay "Silencing in Public Schools" suggests that our demands for silence "permeate classroom life so primitively as to make irrelevant the lived experiences, passions, concerns, communities, and biographics" (p. 158). I interpret Fine's "primitive" as a root characteristic, deep-seated and immutable. It is precisely to mute passion and to reduce the relevance of outside-of-school lives that silence becomes so necessary to schools. While Fine is focused on the specifics of life for low-income, minority students, the same argument can be made regarding the specifics of teachers' personal lives. From my perspective, silencing is also effectively used to control teachers' lives both inside and outside of school. Teachers and students enter a no-talk zone, where our passions are inappropriate. Yet we are encouraged to be passionate about the education of our students. So passion, like silence, is selective and ambiguous. The ambiguity that characterizes our passion in school contexts is something that our silences contain. And silence, which is used to denote absence, is never able to fulfill its mission. Existence can't tolerate a vacuum; and with nothing being said, our desires and our passions fester. In effect, with silence we foreground the expectation that our desires will, can, and do manifest in schools.

Psychoanalysts call this need to locate our desire outside of ourselves projective identification. As Carpy (1989) writes, "Projective identification is a primitive phenomenon and can therefore only involve very powerful feelings which are only able to be dealt with in this way [projection] because the patient is unable to put them in words" (p. 287). That projective identifications are characteristic of erotic transferences makes them tougher to explore. Wrye and Welles (1994) contend that the "erotic component can be the last of which the patient, the therapist, or the supervisor becomes aware" (p. 68). The silencing of teachers' sexual desires, therefore, can lead to distortions and compromise formations of those silenced desires. What is silenced and transferred comes back to us in exoticized, commodified forms. Thus projecting a healthy desire for children to a site within gay men hypersexualizes homosexuality and desexualizes teachers. It is an exchange that ill serves both parties.

Of course, transferring desire onto someone else does not quench it. Desire flourishes in displacement. Desire is always ignorant of its true object. Projecting teachers' desires onto gay men works to hide but not to diminish the strength of teachers' attachments to children. The desire, which is now located in gay men, still operates within the teacher. What began as a teacher's attachment to children, an attachment that is potentially productive and healthy, is transferred to some Other, a site of constructed pathology.

Denying Desire, Denying Self

There are also other ways to interpret the intentions and purposes behind silenced discourses of desire. Silence can be the language of denial. Arguing from Lacan, Walkerdine (1990) suggests that in silence and denial about what is different, we find our own desires. Denial makes the production of desire possible. It appears to be a double bind. First, desire (sexuality) is the thing that cannot be discussed. Yet the denial of desire is the very production of it. When we establish difference—that is, what is not part of us—there is the potential, if not the intent, of making exotic that constructed difference; that is, an occasion for our desire. According to Walkerdine (1990), it is the simultaneous denial of desire and denial of self, in contrast with the production of desire in the service of the "developing child," that make teaching young children an irrational project. While gay men in particular and sexual orientation in general would seem minor ingredients in such a salty soup, a wider look at women's desire may suggest otherwise.

Butler (1990) argues against the Lacanian notion that women's experience, especially their sexualities, are framed by their performance (masquerade) of what the man is not. In order to instantiate (for the male) what it means to be a male, women perform "not male" to define men's masculinity. "The masquerade is what women do to participate in man's desire, but at the cost of giving up their own" (p. 47). In contrast, Butler argues that such a masquerade also creates the possibility for a pre-performative female sexuality—or at the least relegates Lacanian notions of women's gender performance to a "parotic (de)-construction" of men's desire. Both Walkerdine's direct description of women's self-displacement in teaching and Butler's arguments for women's sexual displacement have implications for men's participation in women's teaching space.

The systematic displacement of desire and of self is basic to both the construction of teaching and to the construction and maintenance of beliefs about culture in which teaching is embedded. Thus enacting the role of elementary teacher may be a different experience for males and females, even when the behaviors and intentions behind them appear to be identical.

Teaching Is (More) Women's Work

For some, then, teaching children during their early years is synonymous with caring. Yet to be the one caring is enacted at some personal cost.

For Walkerdine (1990), the teacher–mother functions as the container of irrationality. As the primary grade teacher instantiates social control into the minds of young children, she also shunts her own person out of the picture to make way for the "developing child." Like the worker bee who cleans and feeds the larvae, teachers are to serve children's needs. But simultaneously, these needs are not desires. An innocent and vacuous child having desire is unthinkable. Similarly, teachers constructed in this Victorian-classroom mold can have no desire. In fact, McWilliam (1995) has argued that teachers have been severed from their bodies. Without bodies, without desire, teachers can be frozen in a revered state, put in the cloakroom at the end of schoolday, and be made to stay single, stay childless, and stay away when they were visibly pregnant.

Why have we created this separation of care and desire that prohibits teachers touching children? In her analysis of Samuel Johnson's mid-eighteenth-century writings on morality and imagination, Spacks (1990) suggests that for Johnson "desire's power, derived from the dangerous prevalence of imagination, depends on the human tendency to project into the future. To resist the power of the imagined future almost exceeds human capacity" (p. 19). For Dr. Johnson, desire (regardless of its object) must be governed and resisted. Desire is part of nature, which is base and in need of regulation. The eighteenth- and nineteenth-century models of virginal, asexual teachers may have been superseded by modernist versions of woman and teacher, but we have not fully rejected the previous century's notion of teachers as disembodied, desexualized care providers.

PERMISSIBLE TEACHERS: A SUMMARY

Even while many males, gay and straight, are providing rich, moral, and appropriate classrooms for young children, their identities as constructed by others are being used to keep additional men out of primary education. Further, while the interrogation of male sexuality and its relationship to care is not limited to gay males (cf. N. Segal, 1992), the current focus on homosexuality is taken from the perspectives of the primary grade male teachers in this study, both gay and straight.

Because of general comfort with the notion of a disembodied teacher, and given the deeply rooted homophobic tenor of our culture, gay men provide a ready vessel for our deferred desire. Gay men carry the desire we all feel for young children. I am not suggesting that parents or teachers want to engage sexually with children. Nor am I suggesting that men—gay or straight—want that relationship either. I am pointing out that our culture is projecting the sensual attachments we all have to children onto the figure of the homosexual.

Within a homophobic stereotype, which constructs me as a self-centered, sexual predator, how can I participate in the intense social interactions that comprise the intimacy of classroom relationships? Rather than attacking the social wisdom that undergirds these falsehoods, we are all silent. We don't talk about sexual desire, especially the desire of a gay adult male. Our response to not hiring gay and lesbian teachers has been "better safe than sorry." To push an insidious question to its absurd limits, how can we allow anyone with a history of carnal thoughts to associate with children, who are constructed as innocent? If our answer remains "better safe than sorry," children will have no teachers, male or female, gay or nongay.

CHAPTER 13

Reframing the Choices:
Lessons Learned from
Primary Grade Male Teachers

This final chapter examines the major themes of care, gender, and sexual orientation from more complex vantage points. One lesson about these concepts and their relationship to primary grade teaching is their complexity and interrelatedness. In the teaching lives of these participants, these perspectives are interwoven. The discussions in previous chapters, however, intentionally segmented them. As a way to reintegrate them, this chapter reviews the categories that were used to define the men's teaching in the primary grades.

THE COMPLEXITY OF CATEGORIZING

The complexity of the men's descriptions of their work is reflected in our struggles to describe that work and revealed in the number of metaphors that we used to talk about their teaching. As discussed in previous chapters, their view of themselves as primary teachers was consistently one of comparison with their female colleagues. However, using a lens such as feminism, or care, or gender, or effective teaching not only isolates a phenomenon but also brings much connotative meaning within the lens. These culturally loaded perspectives present problems of interpretation when bias and agenda invade the descriptions. These interpretive problems are not unlike the dilemmas faced by poststructuralist theorists in educational culture (Giroux, 1996), who also seek to avoid the deceptive simplicity of one-word, categorical explanations. Our provisional solution to describing our work without being defined by the limits of the descriptors was a relative one. We consistently defined and redefined our constructs in relation to other constructs that emerged in the study.

It makes little sense to define a construct such as discipline as something that exists outside of a social context. Therefore, discipline was multiply understood from recursive perspectives of care, of feminism, of masculinity, as well as other views. Likewise, we understood teachers' caring in terms of their teaching behaviors, their biological sex, and the intentions for the care of children that motivated the behavior. I am mindful of Bubeck's (1995) relativist critique of Gilligan's view of women's connected morality. But relativism is itself a social construction, and relativism in the use of social categories is something that Minh-Ha (1991) has suggested might be particularly productive for dealing with identity politics in a postmodern culture. It is not that the men in the study claim not to be masculine but that they can respond to a phenomenon in their teaching from either inside or outside a masculine frame of reference. Minh-Ha makes the insider/outsider issue an optional and purposeful stance. Participants can choose a variety of perspectives from which to assemble an interpretation. The male primary teachers may provisionally claim to have a marginalized view inside teaching, a female-dominated culture. But they must also recognize that their claims of marginality are less credible from a broader view of the culture outside of education, one that is largely male-dominated. As discussed in Chapter 10, the men characteristically maneuver into an "effective teaching" category to discuss behavior that they desire as teachers but may resist as males.

Yet the match between the men's use of constructs such as gender and my analysis of them was not a direct one. In the previous example, claiming expertise in a certain behavior (e.g., soft talking through conflicts) because it is good teaching doesn't appear to invoke a gender dichotomy. But the ways that the men characteristically framed this talk revealed their preoccupation with issues of gender. For example, to talk about touch, participants would first acknowledge that women were permitted this behavior because it was female. Then the attribution was repudiated with "just good teaching," and the behavior was recovered for use by male teachers. Gender and care were frequently co-constructed in this way. Similar examples for many other teaching strategies and competencies appeared in the data from the primary grade male teachers. The participants' relative positioning of themselves with respect to categorical frames such as touch and female was consistent and led them to utilize two perspectives (e.g., care and gender) simultaneously. Though the male teachers did not engage in critical analyses of their own work, such analysis is not beyond others' perspectives.

CARING AS A MATERIAL OBJECT

In my view, care can be seen as a performance of gender; that is, care and service work are most often women's work. Accepting such a dubious benediction maintains women's subordinated work status. Working within this context, men can be seen as test cases in disrupting that subordination.

Yet care is a multiply envisioned construct. Therefore, entering what I have labeled a "caring context" does not necessarily mean that all participants perform these intentions to care in similar ways. Caring may manifest in caring for or caring about, according to Tronto (1993). Care may also be invisible or have the appearance of not caring. And care may be absent in appearance *and* intention during a teacher's constructions of interactions with students. Into this complexity of possibilities, all construed with the understanding that "all (primary) teachers (should) care," enter these men who do intend to care but find it difficult to do so.

While the gender of caring is female, these male persons are constructed as masculine. Therefore, enacting caring-for behavior, which is seen to involve listening, speaking softly, touching children, and providing space, may be seen as "unnatural acts" for males. Men may also distance themselves from caring for their students, and only care about them. Such teachers may advocate for their students, represent them, and discuss them with others. Men may also appear not to care. It is striking that the options for care are identical for men and women, but the choices are weighted differently based on gender. Within an established profession such as teaching, why is gender assignment more substantial than competence, ability, experience, or wisdom?

How is it that these gender-based relationships of social and work roles are maintained such that women are viewed as "appropriate" and men as "inappropriate" teachers for the primary grades? In critiquing Noddings's (1984) model of caring, Bubeck (1995) points out that for Noddings, resolutions for ethical dilemmas in caring are context-bound. Bubeck points out the internal paradox in Noddings's approach to care. In Noddings's discussion, the parameters for caring are necessarily tied to each example that is given, that is, they are context-bound. Yet the "ethic of care" offered by Noddings is intended as a universal. In order to avoid this conundrum identified by Bubeck, the larger social forces that impinge on the men who teach in the primary grades are offered.

Graham (1983) succinctly identifies the paradox in professional caring in her title "Caring as a Labor of Love." Care is construed both materially (work, activity, burden) and psychologically (emotions, feelings, involvement). The dual natures of care thus defined help to explain the ambiguity of care that may relegate it to a subordinated status. The social aspects of care locate it within the personal, whereas the economic aspects relegate care to the status of unpaid labor. "Because caring is gendered, these relations of obligation are fundamentally bound up with the subservient position of women" (Thomas, 1993, p. 659).

According to Bubeck (1995), however, "care does not have to be unpaid care" (p. 131, note 12). Bubeck reasons that "if caring is done for others, it follows . . . that it benefits people other than the carer herself. It thus involves an asymmetrical transaction of material benefits" (p. 139). This is an important point, because it opens the argument for economic theorizing that involves the exploitation of women as carers. Bubeck (1995) continues:

> Unless the carer is remunerated in some way (in kind or paid), or the care she gives is reciprocated, she incurs a material net burden. . . . It is this characteristic of care that makes those who tend to take it on vulnerable to exploitation. (pp. 139–141)

According to Adkins (1995), the relationship of women (as workers) to care (the work) is one predicated on a more general relationship of "men's control over women's access to paid work [which] acts as a key mechanism through which women's dependency upon men is maintained" (p. 24). Hartmann (1979) suggests that "job segregation by sex . . . is the primary mechanism in capitalist society that maintains the superiority of men over women, because it enforces lower wages onto women in the labour market" (p. 208). Adkins (1995) concurs, adding the final perspective that control of job access is "central to the formation of gender, that is the social production of men and women" (p. 28) and, even more directly, "gender is produced by the sexual division of labour" (p. 28).

Adkins's argument is based on an extensive study of British leisure/service work, in which service behaviors are treated as a commodity that is assigned to women. The material worth of women's service work is less valued than the work of men who manage women's service efforts. The consistency of these findings with those previously presented in Chapter 1 for teaching and for nursing is sobering. Such regularity in remuneration for gender-differentiated competency suggests that larger social forces are at work.

It is reasonable to conclude that there is more at stake here than the sanctity of individual teachers' (male or female) gender assignment. Rather, gender and its use are being appropriated in primary grade teaching to reproduce economic relations that privilege men's work while devaluing women's. Yet the site of this contest is the individual teacher. And further, we teachers are participating in this use of gender as an economic lever.

The participants in this study used teaching behavior from both sides of the gender chasm. But borrowing across gender boundaries incurs a debt that is accrued with others' interests. The male primary teachers operated within a double frame. They realized that their teaching work was potentially devalued outside the school context because they were males. Yet inside the school, they insisted that their teaching work be valued at least as much as the work of their female colleagues. Further, they sometimes devalued their colleagues' work in order to enhance the value of their own. Inside accusations also devalued the performance of the performer. In several instances, participants expressed concern about effeminacy displayed by other participants in the study. Outside the study and in the larger culture, all of the participants were subject to the same devaluing ("If he does crafts, he must be gay").

We heard these judgments as border patrols that affected our work together. And as revealed by Adkins (1995), Bubeck (1995), Hartmann (1979), and Reskin (1991), one intent of such patrol is to contain our incursion into the economic balance of patriarchal relations, relations that require static gender roles, enforce compulsory heterosexuality, and vilify homosexuality.

It is especially troubling to me that as a group we had some internal difficulties with sexual difference. Two participants were surprised that so much of the talk during the focus group centered on gay teachers. One participant suggested that he was not comfortable with "a lot of gay focus" in the final manuscript. I understand this dissonance as internalized border patrols that monitor who can be teachers and what we can discuss.

Our caring for children, and for each other, continues to be a learned behavior. Our group time was short. It seems productive to convene additional groups with additional teachers in order to discuss our lives as "primary grade male teachers." And as we come together to talk, the talk itself must be talked about. Two aspects of gender and language interplay occurred recursively in this study. The first was men's linguistic competence and their relative match to the ways women were thought to communicate in their schools. The second issue was the use of language as a material object and men's abilities and/or willingness to manipulate it.

MY THINKING ABOUT MEN'S TALKING ABOUT WOMEN'S TALKING

To better understand the reactions that the men who taught in the primary grades had toward communication patterns in the workplace, it is helpful to look at the ways others have described communication as gendered behavior. A similarly essentialist point of view is proposed by the popular linguist Deborah Tannen (1994), who suggests that there are patterned differences between the ways of talking that are primarily located in gender. Tannen (1990) is careful to point out that women's conversational styles (as well as men's) are not exclusively available to women and that men are certainly able to participate in women's ways of talking. But, for the most part, patterns of talk that have been associated with women are most frequently and most comfortably performed and understood within gender boundaries.

On the one hand, Tannen's arguments can be seen as supporting the conclusions made by the men in the study. Conversational style differences do exist between genders. Yet, from a constructivist viewpoint, the categories of gender as well as the conversational behaviors attributed to them are also subject to question. Tannen (1994) makes the case that even objectively defined conversational signs, such as silence and interruption, which have traditionally been used as dichotomous oppositions that frame female/male discourse, are themselves subjective constructions. They have no fixed reality or even inherent meanings. Rather, Tannen demonstrates that interruption (also called overlap) can be supportive and auxiliary as well as competitive and dominant. Both silences and oblique references can be used to control conversation in addition to being manifestations of powerlessness. Rather than fixing on a particular strategy to determine communicative competence or individuals' styles, the communication issue, or topic, and the reciprocal perception of the others' repertoire all co-construct the shifting power base in the interaction. More important, Tannen argues that the modeling of cultural differences between genders does not necessarily undermine the potential to use that constructed difference as a tool for domination or, in this case, devaluing.

The pattern visible in the male primary grade teachers' understanding of their colleagues' linguistic competence is that the men have it both ways. On one hand, they value women's talk when it is analyzed in relation to children; on the other hand, they critique that same talk in a context with other adults, male or female. It seems to me an example of linguistic diversity as difference or specialness, as well as linguistic difference as a precursor to dominance. This argument is not unlike Gilligan's (1982) theory of women's morality. It is not the assertion that men can't think or talk like women. Rather, it is that they tend not to, and doing so requires learning and concentration for most men.

For Tannen (1990), troubles talk is a way of maintaining cohesion and connection in the relationship. Yet the implicit linguistic contract in troubles talk is reciprocity. If I share "a small secret" with you, I anticipate that you will respond in kind. My own experiences have shown me that there is some stylistic variation here. Some teachers choose from their repertoire of personal narratives more effectively than others when sharing their troubles. For example, in addition to solidarity, I may also work toward empathy, or contrast, or alternative interpretations with my choice of a "small secret." My choosing can reveal my intention or position relative to my partner in speaking.

For men who are simply trying to get along with, share ideas with, and understand their colleagues, the subtleties presented by Tannen in descriptions of troubles talk and by Spacks (1985) in accounts of gossip seem daunt-

ing. This understanding is hard work, dearly acquired and closely monitored. But learning and using women's ways of talking seems a reasonable
aptitude for productive work in a primary grade teaching context. What
seems like a likely first step is to accommodate to the fact that gender-based
assumptions are forming our interpretations on both sides of the this chasm.
As the minority group, men are in the political position of "studying up" to
function in the social context they wish to enter. Yet, in the larger social
context, men studying women's practice can also be simultaneously interpreted as "studying down." Men may be seen as voluntary minorities (Ogbu,
1992) when they desire a place in women's work culture. But the habit of
patriarchy is hard to break and a desire to fit in can also drive home the
frustration and impatience. Males living within patriarchal culture can (and
do) assume that our perspective is *the* perspective.

The second perspective on language is its revered status as *the* curriculum of the primary grades. Cal has argued both in Chapter 8 and elsewhere
in this book that women's use of language and text-mediated curriculum is a
patterned response that reveals women's avoidance of autonomy and personal responsibility in their teaching. As examined in Chapter 11, language
instruction fixes reality in a text, where it can be better managed. This,
according to Cal, is in direct contrast to learning from immediate experience.

LANGUAGE ARTS AND GENDER

Cal's arguments regarding gendered curriculum receive some support from
Gilbert (1994). While Gilbert does not question the intent to use language as
a mediation context, she does offer an interesting perspective on gender-
sensitized teaching in the subject area of literacy. She suggests that in the
case of writing we "authorize disadvantage," particularly for young females,
when writing is seen as a natural process:

> Many of the students interviewed had convinced themselves that the reason
> for their lack of success in English was that they were not really "creative" or
> "original" people, and certainly the way in which "creative writing" was
> treated in the classroom did nothing to alter this assumption. (p. 266)

Gilbert makes the point here and elsewhere (Gilbert, 1988) that school litera-
cies privilege masculinist and patriarchal constructions of narratives. In
school writing we prize the individual, the authentic, "the natural, the personal, the spontaneous" (1994, p. 266). What we fail to do, according to
Gilbert, is to directly teach the technical skills that will enhance students'

approximation of what we tacitly prize (textualized masculinity). It is toward this implicit value for the masculine that Gilbert levies her strongest criticism. By valorizing the "authentic expression of an *individual's* own ideas" (Moffett, 1981, cited in Gilbert, 1994, p. 261; emphasis added), we uncritically reinscribe a male voice and authorize disadvantage for female students. Cal and Gilbert are making parallel arguments about language curricula, but from very different perspectives and with opposing intentions. Unlike Cal, Gilbert suggests that text-centered curriculum may disenfranchise young females.

Clough (1992) offers a similar critique of authoring practices and their embedded assumptions in the field of ethnographic texts. Clough (1992) suggests that in its narrative construction of subjectivities, ethnographic narrative displaces the author's desire (or goal orientation) into the production of the narrative. This, according to Clough, allows for a fantasmic construction of a unified subject identity (an other). Once individuation is established, the now-separated other (or object of study) can engage in a struggle for identity, which constitutes the rudiments of a life history. And, then, finally,

> ethnography [narrative] is informed with an oedipal logic of realist narrativity, . . . because ethnography treats the subject's struggle for self-knowledge as a struggle [now the author's] to obtain factual representation of empirical reality. (pp. 26–27)

For teachers, there may be some benefit in recognizing that the production of narratives may be patriarchal (cf. Heilbrun, 1988), whereas the use of narrative or storytelling may seen as "women's ways of knowing."

The common ground in Cal's critique and those offered by Gilbert and Clough is the understanding that language and its use are suffused with gender issues. How language is made, how it is used to confer and keep power, and how it is valued as a commodity or as a pastime are all issues that require recursive attention. While Cal and Gilbert have much in common in their praxis, the paths each has taken are quite different from each other. Gilbert's arguments are made from a poststructuralist, feminist perspective that appears to be advocating for women's increased options with texts. We teach that writers (men) benefit from natural expression of real experience. We don't teach students how to accomplish "natural writing." In contrast, Cal's similar-sounding stance comes from an essentialist argument that maintains the differences between men and women and the ways we enact teaching. Women care (about language) and men teach curriculum (writing). Both stances are/can be productive ones for developing writers. Foucault (1972) is careful to point out the defining and limiting powers inherent in our different discourse collectives. Insider knowledge is connected to the power that preserves the discourse community. It is a circle that repels outsiders' entry. Discourse communities, such as "natural writers," contain the power of the language form by not sharing it with outsiders. Successful writers can be seen as those who do not share. Certainly the talk that delimits a way of knowing is something we must share with the learners. The lesson is important for both elementary classroom practices, which involve young language and literacy learners, and for teachers who are learning professional discourse frames. But a point not addressed by Foucault's description of disciplinary knowledges, nor by Gilbert's arguments about classroom pedagogy in writing, nor by Cal's unrest about women's teaching fixation on language, is the situatedness and parallel realities of men's and women's talk and ways of knowing. It is risky business to cross the gender-patrolled borders of language. In addition to language access, other issues of power and control were used to describe the teaching of the men in this study. While there was much resistance to requests for their disciplining of students, there was only limited questioning of what was meant by "disciplining."

DISCIPLINARY REGULATION

Teachers' intentions to discipline or refusal to do so are complex decisions made within larger frames—among them, gender and authority. The men in this study reported a variety of responses to the call to discipline. Whether they chose to intervene or to wait for the child to develop the desired behaviors, their choice had an impact. Walkerdine (1990) has characterized much early education work as passive waiting for the development of children. In a discussion of two preschool boys' resistance to control by their female teacher, Walkerdine shows in dialogue how the boys resisted their teacher by referring to her body parts and her underwear in sexist ways.

> The sequence begins when Annie [3 years] takes a piece of Lego to add on a construction she is building. Terry [4 years] tries to take it away from her to use himself, and she resists. He says:
>
> TERRY: You're a stupid cunt, Annie.
>
> The teacher [Miss Baxter] tells him to stop and Sean [4 years] tries to mess up another child's construction. The teacher tells him to stop. Then Sean says:
>
> SEAN: Get out of it Miss Baxter paxter.
> TERRY: Get out of it knickers Miss Baxter.

SEAN: Get out of it Miss Baxter paxter.

TERRY: Get out of it Miss Baxter the knickers paxter knickers, bum.

SEAN: Knickers, shit, bum.

MISS B: Sean, that's enough, you're being silly.

SEAN: Miss Baxter, knickers, show you're knickers.

TERRY: Miss Baxter, show your bum off.

   (they giggle)

MISS B: I think you're being very silly.

TERRY: Shit Miss Baxter, shit Miss Baxter.

SEAN: Miss Baxter, show your knickers your bum off.

SEAN: Take all your clothes off, your bra off.

TERRY: Yeah, and take your bum off, take your wee-wee off, take your clothes, your mouth off.

SEAN: Take your teeth out, take your head off, take your hair off, take your bum off. Miss Baxter the paxter the knickers taxter.

MISS B: Sean, go and find something else to do please. (Walkerdine, 1990, p. 4)

Yet, when queried, the teacher did not see the same sexism that is apparent to many readers (including Walkerdine) in the text. Rather, the teacher understood the boys' "language" as a developmental expectancy. To understand this difference in interpretation, Walkerdine suggests that the boys and the teacher occupy several subject positions simultaneously. She shows how at a given moment participants can be seen occupying those spaces. The boys can be seen as occupying slots for "student," "younger," and "male"—to name only the obvious. In contrast, their teacher is "teacher," "older," and "female." Walkerdine's concern is that in choosing to interpret from *a* frame, in this case developmentalism, the teacher may lose meaning from other perspectives (e.g., feminism). In this case, the boys' comments to another student ("You're a stupid cunt, Annie") and to their teacher ("Miss Baxter, show your bum off") are rationalized as "natural." In both of these examples, Walkerdine shows how 4- and 5-year-old boys have learned how to use sexual synecdoche to control females' behavior. Further, she presents what can be interpreted as their teacher's collusion in their performance of sexism.

For young girls, Walkerdine (1990) presents their control as purposeful manipulation of classroom social interactions toward the domestic, where, she reasons, they have situated power and recognize it. Elsewhere, Walkerdine (1996a,b) examines the relative costs of such power. Of interest here is how teachers' awareness of the influence of gender in their own teaching informs, or could inform, teaching decisions. What are the moral constraints that inform teachers' choices when they engage with their students on issues of gender expectations? How do teachers' personal definitions of caring precipitate behaviors toward children for whom they intend to care? How do teachers' gender beliefs and performances of those beliefs impact their teaching?

For me, it is not productive to use the preceding example as one of "shoulds." Nor do I think Walkerdine's intent was to do so. Rather, viewing the circumstances with the complexity they deserve is my goal. It is an example of exactly why others can't tell teachers what is and what is not appropriate practice. These are the decisions of individual teachers as we navigate the social constructions of our multiple selves with our students in countless such situations. Nor are our decisions above criticism and questioning. These decisions are most productively made within a teacher, with other teachers, and without the pressure of (pre)scripted performances.

Using Foucault's (1977) arguments, Walkerdine (1990) proposes that "democracy" in schools is based on normalization of behaviors into predictable patterns. Schooling is the site of the development of normalization, or the social approximation of "natural development." The cost of instantiating "natural development" is borne by the teacher who, like the mother, waits passively for development.

> She is the servant of the omnipotent child, whose needs she must meet at all times. . . . His majesty, the baby becomes his highness the child. The price of autonomy [for children] is woman. . . . The servicing labor of women makes the child, the natural child, possible. (Walkerdine, 1990, p. 24)

Walkerdine (1990) further elaborates:

> [To be] fit only for maternal nurturance is something which . . . pathologizes activity and passion. Needs replace desire. Affect replaces libido . . . it is masculine sexuality, to the point of violence, which is validated by this pedagogy. It is the female teacher who is to contain this transformation which turns physical violence into the symbolic violence of mastery, the law. And in each case, the woman, as container, soaks up and contains the irrationality which she best understands. (p. 24)

Part of the boundary crossing for males who enter this space is an awareness of the positionings that women hold in the production of rationality. Their outside-in perspectives require that the men who desire to work in this space have some understandings of why things work like they do. Suspension of desire, of self, can involve very different acts, with different costs for men and women. While Walkerdine's depiction of a self-effacing female teacher "fits" into some preconfigured slot for "teacher," those same behaviors, performed by males with identical intentions, may be read as weak, sneaky, or even depraved. I do not understand Walkerdine to mean that men can't "soak it up." However, this self-effacement is conceivably understood in different ways by men and by those who watch them.

Believing in their own autonomy, men may be less predisposed to nurture the development of the children. This argument goes deeper than the construction of the "rules of discipline." It engages at the level of teachers' beliefs about children's constructions of power, knowledge, and relationships. It is paradoxical that from a progressive perspective, child-centered female teachers would view men as having "an easier time with controlling kids" when the ideal of progressive education is students' internalized control, or self-regulation. Yet, in resisting discipline by force or by authority, a male could also engender resentment for betraying the patriarchal bargain. It could also be that men would be exceedingly ill equipped and frustrated as teachers of young children when self-regulation is a goal. It is also problematic to locate these sensibilities as the domain of one gender. Nurturance and caring are thus reinscribed as women's work, and power and control the work of men.

Progressive, child-centered education does not overtly control children. Rather, the control is located inside the learner. In child-centered pedagogy, freedom is taken to mean the apparent absence of control by the teacher. Oyler (1996) points out that teachers can also be viewed as using more subtle means of power in classrooms that only appear to avoid control. Of course, the focus in this example is on what the students experience and what teachers believe to be in operation. But what this celebration of freedom conceals is the personal costs to teachers in moving children to self-regulation through reason and rationality. Part of the border crossing for males who enter this female space is our continued awareness of our difference in positions of personal agency that men and women vacate in their production of rational children. Viewed in this way, the protected social context of elementary schools, and especially primary grade classrooms, can be seen as a crucible for the alchemy of patriarchy. What does it mean for men to attempt this work? How can we make this space one that reinvents constructs such as discipline and gender?

Some of the female teachers who were the study participants' colleagues viewed them as having an easier time controlling kids. This is based on the assumption that male teachers are more comfortable wielding authority. Investing male teachers with the power to discipline is not congruent with current philosophy about child-centered pedagogy. Further, such understanding, constructed along gender lines, reinscribes power and control in male teachers and nurturing exclusively in female teachers. We need to move beyond such gender binaries. Like the bilingual teacher in an ESOL classroom, teachers with a foot on each side of the gender chasm can be productive resources. Granted, such gendered teaching and the requisite reconceptualization of constructs such as discipline would fall under what Britzman (1992) has characterized as "unpopular discourses." But feminist educational theorists hammer home the necessity of pursuing unpopular discourses (Barrs & Pidgeon, 1994; Christian-Smith, 1993; Gilbert, 1980, 1994; Walkerdine, 1990).

Some of this work must be initiated by men who have chosen to work with women, doing "women's work." After all, as apprentices, we are learners. In contrast to our relative comfort with autonomy, men may be less able to empathize with children's needs for their own autonomy and identity struggles. This argument engages teachers at the level of our beliefs about children's constructions of power, knowledge, and relationships. In contrast, for gay men who have experienced masculinity as a performance (Simpson, 1994), these shifts in perspective that are required for self-denial may be done with some experience. Of course, recognizing these social facts as analogous to women's displacement is not a cause for mindless celebration. Sensitivity to others' needs for autonomy can be seen as a by-product of lives, male and female, lived in response to patriarchy. It is my belief that gay men, who have lived the construction (and deconstruction) of gender on a daily basis, may be ideally positioned to understand the identity confusion and struggles of young children.

MEN, SEX, AND TEACHING

While I am arguing for the inclusion of men as elementary teachers, others reason that we are unsuitable *because* of our male sexual persona; quite oppositely, others believe that those who even *act* like homosexuals should not be allowed to teach. I owe what understanding I have of children and teaching to the feminine parts of my personality. I learned these things as women do, sitting in the kitchen, listening to stories, babysitting, and caring about and for others. These preparatory experiences are ones that other teachers have as well. I also think my knowledge is related to my sexual orientation. I think of myself as a male who is apprenticing in feminism. I have had access to women's lives and stories in ways that are unique because I am less likely to be seen as a sexual predator. Yet this learning is not available in a public way. Perhaps men's covert use of women's perspective keeps it a limited and valued commodity, while not upsetting the economy of the early education sweatshop. I will only know when *what* I know and *how* I know it are not whispered behind a fan of fingers and not told with eyes that ricochet from side to side.

Adult behaviors, such as patting, touching, and hugging, are all female until they are performed by males, at which point they are "marked," or conspicuous. Our response to others' marking of our behavior has elicited a series or rationalized, compromise formations for our teaching behavior. It is, for example, less risky for me to touch a child if "there is a reason." With a tissue to wipe a nose, the fingers that will tie a shoe, the hands that adjust the hat, I am simply using tools to do a job. I feel less secure when I pat or touch a child to show my caring or because *I* might need that contact. Women kiss and hug their young students. I've seen them. It seemed very normal to me. But, of course, I can't. The second message is that I shouldn't want to. Nor can a young girl or boy sit on my lap. My caution is an internalized knowledge that others suspect that a squirming butt on my lap might be a cause for my sexual arousal. This kind of thinking is interesting because it does not occur to me when I work with children. It is only when I think about others' concerns with my teaching of young children that these problematic relationships even occur to me. Naming these presuppositions is an exercise in filling in the unarticulated fears of others. In her discussion of realist ethnography, Clough (1992) offers an explanation that can be generalized beyond textual accounts of interpretation. She writes:

> Realist accounts, whether they be of race, class, ethnicity, gender, or national-ity, put into play unconscious fantasy. These accounts not only present the "facts" but in so doing, they publicize fantasies that authorize the facts as realities. (p. 12)

For this study, the circulation of stories that male teachers in the primary grades were pedophiles, and that gay teachers were also pedophiles, not only made "facts" of these constructions but also made public the uncon-scious desires of the storytellers. Where we teachers locate our sexual de-sires is of great interest and consequence to the parents of the children we teach. But parents' motives and the intent of commercial enterprises who exploit those motives remain problems that we "can't talk about."

Logically, parents' concerns about teachers' sexuality are centered on the potential for teachers' sexual involvement with their children. In a proac-tive stance, parents also carefully monitor the *potential* for the involvement of their children in inappropriate sexual scenarios. But this is exactly where projections, all of ours, about individuals' identities come into play. When parents of young children mistakenly believe that male primary grade teach-ers are necessarily homosexual, or pedophilic, or both, the implications are disastrous.

When a parent suspects that his son's teacher is gay, and that being gay is a predisposition to sexual desire for children, then the teacher's behaviors, *all* of them, are likely to be interpreted from a prefigured sexual stance. In this situation, all touch is suspect. Any attention can be seen as inappropriate. Publicized accusations of impropriety, which may emanate from reasonable teaching touch, are sufficient to end a teaching career. Teachers I know who have been snared in this web have been counseled to plea bargain. Professional teachers are being advised by lawyers, who are retained by teacher unions, to enter a plea of "inappropriate touch without criminal intent." The teachers agree to relinquish their teaching positions and certification.

The rationale used to support this tacit admission of culpability is one forged in pragmatics, not ethics. Since the teacher is likely "known to be gay," his chances of withstanding scrutiny are slim to none. Presumably, the material fact that a teacher is homosexual is sufficient to forestall any counterargument to the unjust accusations of "inappropriate touch." These are not isolated or unusual cases. "Resolutions" such as these are more frequent than we even suspect. This is because they are purposefully constructed to avoid public scrutiny. From my perspective, it is necessary to begin discussing teachers' dilemmas that result from others' speculations about teachers' desires, life partners, marital status, and living circumstances. It is unjust to extort teachers into guilty silence about their lives.

The pressures for teachers to be asexual and to defer to men and children are strong in elementary education. Caring as a way of knowing for females has been criticized for reproducing a male/female moral reasoning dichotomy and for essentializing females' character traits (Broughton, 1983; Code, 1991). Further, Tronto (1993) describes care as a morality born of subordination. Teachers, especially teachers of young children, care, but not about themselves. They are passionate, but only about children's lives. They make themselves into vessels for children's lives by emptying themselves of desire. We may know individual teachers to be self-protective and self-indulgent. But the disembodied, idealized category of teacher defers her desire.

The elementary teacher—always presumed to be female—is praised for deferring her personal desire to the needs of the emerging child. But such selfless behavior is systematically devalued in a sexist, patriarchal culture. Because "care" is axiomatic in elementary teaching, and because it is believed to be "natural" for females, the work is seen as unskilled and genetic, rather than technical or learned. With "care" located within constructions of femininity, men are constructed as "at risk" for providing care. We are at risk because we are not female and, therefore, cannot be caring. Or we are at risk because we cannot be caring without being sexual. Or we are at risk because if we can be caring without being sexual, we upset the economy that traps female teachers in an early education sweatshop. If care is naturally female, then work differentiation based on care, which is necessary for lowering the prestige and value of women's work (Reskin, 1991), is a "naturally occurring" phenomenon. If men claim that they also care, they risk identifying themselves as "unnatural." Some men *are* recognized for their abilities to care. With careers in caring, these men constitute a threat to gendered work differentiation.

Teachers can either be committed or uncommitted to their caring for children. Their construction of teaching as caring is based on their own philosophies about learning and about children. Biological sex as well as sexual orientation have evidently little to do with whether or not men are or can be effective as primary teachers. Socially constructed gender roles and their effective deployment *are* teaching. It is, therefore, others' use of their own perceptions of caring and their automatic suspicions about men's acts of caring that are the real problem with men in primary teaching. My social constructions for "teacher" and "one caring" are constantly under revision, and it is that complex, multilayered understanding about gendered behavior, professional role expectations, and intention behind acts of caring that is in need of continuous investigation. Caring for children in our teaching is something that we constantly build, monitor, and reshape based on the evolving relationship between the "one caring" and the "one cared for." At this time, part of that construction for men who do choose to teach young children is awareness of what others are making of our caring.

References

Adkins, L. (1995). *Gendered work: Sexuality, family and the labour market.* Buckingham, UK: Open University Press.

Agar, M. (1980). *The professional stranger: An informal introduction to ethnography.* New York: Academic Press.

Anderson, S. (1966). *Winesburg, Ohio.* New York: Viking. (Original work published 1919)

Barrs, M., & Pidgeon, S. (Eds.). (1994). *Reading the difference: Gender and reading in elementary classrooms.* York, ME: Stenhouse.

Batchelor, E., Dean, R., Gridley, B., & Batchelor, B. (1990). Reports of child sexual abuse in the schools. *Psychology in the Schools, 27,* 131–137.

Belenky, M., Clinchy, B., Goldberger, N., & Tarule, J. (1986). *Women's ways of knowing: The development of self, voice, and mind.* New York: Basic Books.

Benhabib, S. (1987). The generalized and the concrete other: The Kohlberg–Gilligan controversy and feminist theory. In S. Benhabib and D. Cornell (Eds.), *Feminism as critique: On the politics of gender* (pp. 77–95). Minneapolis: University of Minnesota Press.

Bogdan, R., & Biklen, S. (1992). *Qualitative research for education: An introduction to theory and methods* (2nd ed.). Boston: Allyn & Bacon.

Boswell, J. (1984). *Christianity, social tolerance, and homosexuality: Gay people in Western Europe from the beginning of the Christian era to the fourteenth century.* Chicago: University of Chicago Press.

Boswell, J. (1994). *Same-sex unions in premodern Europe.* New York: Villard.

Bradley, H. (1993). Across the great divide: The entry of men into women's jobs. In C. Williams (Ed.), *Doing "women's work": Men in nontraditional occupations* (pp. 10–27). Newbury Park, CA: Sage.

Britzman, D. (1992). Decentering discourses in teacher education: Or, the unleashing of unpopular things. In K. Weiler & C. Mitchell (Eds.), *What schools can do: Critical pedagogy and practice* (pp. 151–175). Albany: State University of New York Press.

Brophy, J., & Good, T. (1973a). Feminization of American public schools. *Phi Delta Kappan, 54,* 564–566.

Brophy, J., & Good, T. (1973b). Of course the schools are feminine, but let's stop blaming women for it. *Phi Delta Kappan, 55,* 73–75.

Broughton, J. (1983). Women's rationality and men's virtues. *Social Research, 50,* 597–642.

Browning, F. (1993). *The culture of desire: Paradox and perversity in gay lives today.* New York: Crown.

Bubeck, D. (1995). *Care, gender, and justice.* Oxford, UK: Oxford University Press.

Butler, J. (1990). *Gender trouble: Feminism and the subversion of identity.* New York: Routledge.

Carpy, D. (1989). Tolerating the countertransference: A mutative process. *International Journal of Psychoanalysis, 70,* 287–294.

Chodorow, N. (1978). *Reproduction of mothering.* Berkeley: University of California Press.

Christian-Smith, L. (Ed.). (1993). *Texts of desire: Essays on fiction, femininity, and schooling.* New York: Falmer.

Clough, P. (1992). *The end(s) of ethnography: From realism to social criticism.* Newbury Park, CA: Sage.

Code, L. (1991). *What can she know? Feminist theory and the construction of knowledge.* Ithaca, NY: Cornell University Press.

Fine, M. (1987). Silencing in public schools. *Language Arts, 64,* 157–174.

Fine, M. (1992). Over dinner: Feminism and adolscent female bodies. In M. Fine (Ed.), *Disruptive voices: The possibilities of feminist research* (pp. 175–203). Ann Arbor: University of Michigan Press.

Fine, M. (1993). Sexuality, schooling, and adolescent females: The missing discourse of desire. In L. Weis & M. Fine (Eds.), *Beyond silenced voices: Class, race, and gender in United States schools* (pp. 75–100). Albany: State University of New York Press.

Finkelhor, D., Williams, L., & Burns, N. (1988). *Nursery crimes: Sexual abuse in day care.* Newbury Park, CA: Sage.

Foucault, M. (1972). *The archeology of knowledge.* New York: Pantheon.

Foucault, M. (1977). *Discipline and punish.* London: Allen Lane.

Foucault, M. (1978). *The history of sexuality. Volume I: An introduction.* New York: Pantheon.

Freire, P. (1968). *Pedagogy of the oppressed.* New York: Seabury.

Galton, M., Simon, B., & Croll, P. (1980). *Inside the primary classroom.* London: Routledge.

Gilbert, P. (1980). Personally (and passively) yours: Girls, literacy and education. *Oxford Review of Education, 15,* 257–265.

Gilbert, P. (1988). Student text as pedagogical text. In S. deCastell, A. Luke, & C. Luke (Eds.), *Language, authority and criticism: Readings in the school textbook* (pp. 234–250). New York: Falmer.

Gilbert, P. (1994). Authoring disadvantage: Authorship and creativity in the language classroom. In B. Stierer & J. Maybin (Eds.), *Language, literacy and learning in educational practice* (pp. 258–276). New York: Open University Press.

Gilligan, C. (1982). *In a different voice: Psychological theory and women's moral development.* Cambridge, MA: Harvard University Press.

Gilligan, C. (1987). Moral orientation and moral development. In E. Kittay & D. Meyers (Eds.), *Women and moral theory* (pp. 19–33). Totowa, NJ: Rowman & Littlefield.

Gilligan, C., Lyons, N., & Hanmer, J. (Eds.). (1990). *Making connections: The relational lives of adolescent girls at Emma Willard School.* Cambridge, MA: Harvard University Press.

Giroux, H. (1996). Youthful bodies, pedagogy, and commercial pleasures. *New Art Examiner, 23*, 16.

Glaser, B., & Strauss, A. (1967). *The discovery of grounded theory: Strategies for qualitative research*. Chicago: Aldine.

Goetz, J., & LeCompte, M. (1992). *Ethnography and qualitative design in educational research* (2nd ed.). New York: Academic Press.

Goffman, E. (1963). *Stigma: Notes on the management of spoiled identity*. New York: Simon & Schuster.

Gold, D., & Reis, M. (1982). Male teacher effects on young children: A theoretical and empirical consideration. *Sex Roles, 8*, 493–513.

Goodman, K. (1986). *What's whole in whole language?* Portsmouth, NH: Heinemann.

Graham, H. (1983). Caring as a labor of love. In J. Finch & D. Groves (Eds.), *A labor of love: Women, work, and care* (pp. 13–30). London: Routledge.

Hargreaves, A. (1991). Contrived collegiality: The micropolitics of teacher collaboration. In J. Blase (Ed.), *The politics of life in schools: Power, conflict, and cooperation* (pp. 46–72). Newbury Park, CA: Sage.

Hartmann, H. (1979). Capitalism, patriarchy, and job segregation by sex. In Z. Eisenstein (Ed.), *Capitalist patriarchy and the case for socialist feminism* (pp. 206–247). New York: Monthly Review Press.

Heilbrun, C. (1988). *Writing a woman's life*. New York: Ballentine.

Henderson, G., & Bibens, R. (1970). *Teachers should care: Social perspectives of teaching*. New York: Harper & Row.

Hesselbart, S. (1977). Women doctors win and male nurses lose. *Sociology of Work and Occupations, 4*, 49–62.

Johnson, R. (1995, April). *Subjectivities and desires of preschool teachers: How a "no touch" policy impacts with our beliefs*. Paper presented at the annual meeting of the American Educational Research Association, San Francisco.

Johnson, R. (1997). The "no touch" policy. In J. Tobin (Ed.), *Making a place for pleasure in early childhood education* (pp. 101–118). New Haven, CT: Yale University Press.

Kincaid, J. (1992). *Child-loving: The erotic child and Victorian culture*. New York: Routledge.

King, J. (1992, April). *Mis/s/appropriation and critical crossdressing: Male perspectives on females' stories about teaching*. Paper presented at the annual meeting of the American Educational Research Association, San Francisco, CA.

King, J. (1997). Keeping it quiet. In J. Tobin (Ed.), *Making a place for pleasure in early childhood education* (pp. 235–250). New Haven, CT: Yale University Press.

King, J., & Barksdale-Ladd, M. A. (1995, November). *Constructivism and dilemma of accuracy: An exploratory study*. Paper presented at the annual meeting of the College Reading Association, Clearwater, FL.

King, J., Danforth, S., Perez, S., & Stahl, N. (1994). Is resistance empowerment? In B. Hayes & K. Camperell (Eds.), *Reading: Putting the pieces together* (Fourteenth Yearbook of the American Reading Forum) (pp. 65–76). Logan, UT: American Reading Forum.

King, J., & Holland, M. (1992, December). *Reciprocal observation of college teaching: Show me yours and I'll show you mine*. Paper presented at the annual meeting of the American Reading Forum, Sarasota, FL.

Kohlberg. L. (1981). *The philosophy of moral development*. San Francisco: Harper & Row.

LeVay, S. (1996). *Queer science: The use and abuse of research into homosexuality*. Cambridge, MA: MIT Press.

Lortie, D. (1975). *School teacher: A sociological study*. Chicago: University of Chicago Press.

Lynn, N., Vaden, A., & Vaden, R. (1975). The challenges of men in a women's world. *Public Personnel Management, 4*, 4–12.

McWilliam, E. (1995, April). *Touchy subjects: Pedagogy, performativity and sexuality in classrooms*. Paper presented at the annual meeting of American Educational Research Association, San Francisco.

Minh-Ha, T. (1991). Outside in inside out. In T. Minh-Ha (Ed.), *When the moon waxes red: Representation, gender, and cultural politics* (pp. 65–78). New York: Routledge.

Nails, D. (1983). Social-scientific sexism. *Social Research, 50*, 643–664.

National Association for the Education of Young Children (NAEYC). (1985). *In whose hands?* (Report #760). Washington, DC: Author.

Nias, J. (1981). "Commitment" and motivation in primary school teachers. *Educational Review, 33*, 181–190.

Nias, J. (1985). Reference groups in primary teaching: Talking listening, and identity. In S. Ball & I. Goodson (Eds.), *Teachers' lives and careers* (pp. 105–119). London: Falmer.

Nias, J. (1989). *Primary teachers talking*. New York: Routledge.

Noddings, N. (1984). *Caring: A feminine approach to ethics and moral education*. Berkeley: The University of California Press.

Noddings, N. (1989). Educating moral people. In M. Brabeck (Ed.), *Who cares?: Theory, research, and educational implications of the ethic of care* (pp. 216–232). New York: Praeger.

Noddings, N. (1992). *The challenge to care in schools: An alternative approach to education*. New York: Teachers College Press.

Ogbu, J. (1992). Understanding cultural diversity and learning. *Educational Researcher, 21*, 5–14.

Owens, C. (1992). Outlaws: Gay men in feminism. In S. Bryson, B. Kruger, & J. Weinstock (Eds.), *Beyond recognition: Representation, power and culture: Craig Owens* (pp. 218–255). Berkeley: University of California Press.

Oyler, C. (1996). *Making room for students: Sharing teacher authority in room 104*. New York: Teachers College Press.

Pinar, W. (1975). Currerre: Toward reconceptualization. In W. Pinar (Ed.), *Curriculum theorizing: The reconceptualists* (pp. 396–414). Berkeley, CA: McCutceon.

Plummer, K. (1991). Understanding childhood sexualities. In T. Sandfort, E. Brongersma, & A. van Naerssen (Eds.), *Male intergenerational intimacy* (pp 231–249). New York: Harrington Park Press.

Puka, B. (1990). The liberation of caring: A different voice for Gilligan's Different Voice. *Hypatia, 55*, 58–82.

Puka, B. (1993). The liberation of caring: A different voice for Gilligan's Different

Voice. In M. Larrabee (Ed.), *An ethic of care: Feminist and interdisciplinary perspectives* (pp. 215–239). New York: Routledge.

Reskin, B. (1991). Bring the men back in: Sex differentiation and the devaluation of women's work. In J. Lorber & S. Farrell (Eds.), *The social construction of gender* (pp. 141–161). Beverly Hills, CA: Sage.

Robinson, B. (1979). Men caring for the young: An androgynous perspective. *The Family Coordinator, 28*, 553–560.

Robinson, B. (1981). Changing views on male early childhood teachers. *Young Children, 36*, 27–32.

Robinson, B. (1986). Men caring for the young: A profile. In R. Lewis & M. Sussman (Eds.), *Men's changing roles in the family* (pp. 151–161). New York: Haworth.

Robinson, B., & Canaday, H. (1978). Sex-role behaviors and personality traits of male day care teachers. *Sex Roles, 4*, 853–865.

Robinson, B., & Flake-Hobson, C. (1979). Androgyny: An essential ingredient for male teachers of young children. *Dimensions, 6*, 49–51.

Robinson, B., Sheen, P., & Flake-Hobson, C. (1978). Sex-stereotyped attitudes of male and female child care workers: Support for androgynous child care. *Child Care Quarterly, 9*, 233–242.

Rofes, E. (1985). *Socrates, Plato, and guys like me: Confessions of gay schoolteacher.* Boston: Alyson.

Sarbin, T. (Ed.). (1983). *Narrative psychology.* New York: Praeger.

Schreiber, S. C. (1979). *Changing places: Men and women in transitional occupations.* Cambridge, MA: MIT press.

Sciarra, D. (1974). Men in young children's lives make a difference. *Child Care Quarterly, 1*, 111–118.

Sedgwick, E. (1985). *Between men: English literature and male homosocial desire.* New York: Columbia University Press.

Segal, B. (1962). Male nurses: A case study in status contradiction and prestige loss. *Social Forces, 41*, 31–38.

Segal, N. (1992). Why can't a good man be sexy? Why can't a sexy man be good? In D. Porter (Ed.), *Between men and feminism* (pp. 35–47). New York: Routledge.

Seifert, K. (1983, April). *Suitability and competence of men who teach young children.* Paper presented at the annual meeting of the American Educational Research Association, Montreal, Canada.

Seifert, K. (1988). Men in early childhood education. In B. Spodek, O. Sarancho, & D. Peters (Eds.), *Professionalism and the early childhood practitioner* (pp. 105–116). New York: Teachers College Press.

Shannon, P. (1989). *Broken promises: Reading instruction in twentieth century America.* South Hadley, MA: Bergin & Garvey.

Silin, J. (1995). *Children, sex, and death: Our passion for ignorance in a time of AIDS.* New York: Teachers College Press.

Simpson, M. (1994). *Male impersonators: Men performing masculinity.* New York: Routledge.

Smith, D. (1973). Yes, American schools are feminized. *Phi Delta Kappan, 54*, 703–704.

Spacks, P. (1985). *Gossip.* Chicago: University of Chicago Press.

Spacks, P. (1990). *Desire and truth: Functions of plot in eighteenth-century English novels.* Chicago: University of Chicago Press.

Spender, D. (1986). *Contemporary women teachers: Balancing school and home.* New York: Longman.

Squirrel, G. (1989). In passing . . . teachers and sexual orientation. In S. Acker (Ed.), *Teachers, gender and careers* (pp. 87–106). New York: Falmer.

Stauffer, R. (1980). *The language experience approach to teaching reading.* New York: Harper & Row.

Sugg, R. (1978). *Motherteacher: The feminization of American education.* Charlottesville, VA: University Press of Virginia.

Tannen, D. (1990). *You just don't understand: Women and men in conversation.* New York: Morrow.

Tannen, D. (1994). *Gender and discourse.* New York: Oxford University Press.

Thomas, C. (1993). De-constructing concepts of care. *Sociology, 27,* 649–669.

Tricket, P., & Susman, E. (1988). Parental perspectives of child-rearing practices in physically abusive and non-abusive families. *Developmental Psychology, 24,* 270–276.

Tronto, J. (1993). *Moral boundaries: A political argument for an ethic of care.* New York: Routledge.

Tubbs, E. (1946). More men in our schools. *School and Society, 63,* 394.

Walkerdine, V. (1990). *Schoolgirl fictions.* London: Verso.

Walkerdine, V. (1996a). Popular culture and the eroticization of little girls. In J. Curran, D. Morley, & V. Walkerdine (Eds.), *Cultural studies and communications* (pp. 323–333). New York: Arnold.

Walkerdine, V. (1996b). Subject to change without notice: Psychology, postmodernity, and the popular. In J. Curran, D. Morley, & V. Walkerdine (Eds.), *Cultural studies and communications* (pp. 96–118). New York: Arnold.

Waller, W. (1932). *The sociology of teaching.* New York: Russell & Russell.

Weeks, J. (1985). *Sexuality and its discontents: Meanings, myths, and modern sexualities.* New York: Routledge.

Whitebook, M., Phillips, D., & Howes, C. (1993). *National childcare staffing study revisited.* Washington, DC: National Center for Early Childhood Workforce.

Woods, P. (1987). Managing the primary teacher's role. In S. Delamont (Ed.), *The primary school teacher* (pp. 120–143). New York: Falmer.

Wrye, H., & Welles, J. (1994). *The narration of desire: Erotic transference and countertransference.* Hillsdale, NJ: Analytic Press.

Index

About the Author

JAMES R. KING is a professor of Childhood/Language Arts/Reading at the University of South Florida in Tampa, where he teaches in literacy and qualitative research methods. He has taught in a span of classrooms from first grade to graduate seminars. His studies with faculty at Western Michigan and West Virginia Universities resulted in two graduate degrees in reading and literacy. He has taught with colleagues at the University of Pittsburgh, Texas Woman's University, and the University of British Columbia. Currently, Dr. King is researching the construction of error and accuracy in writing and reading pedagogy.